BEWARE OF THE DOG

Positive Solutions for Aggressive Behavior in Dogs

Pat Miller, CBCC-KA, CPDT-KA

Dogwise™ Publishing

Wenatchee, Washington U.S.A.

Beware of the Dog
Positive Solutions for Aggressive Behavior in Dogs
Pat Miller, CBCC-KA, CPDT-KA

Dogwise Publishing
A Division of Direct Book Service, Inc.
403 South Mission Street, Wenatchee, Washington 98801
1-509-663-9115, 1-800-776-2665
www.dogwisepublishing.com / info@dogwisepublishing.com

Photos: Clarissa Bergeman, Meg Leader, Lisa Santos, Pat Miller and Paul Miller

Graphic Design: Lindsay Peternell

Library of Congress Cataloging-in-Publication Data
Names: Miller, Pat, 1951 October 14- , author.
Title: Beware of the dog : positive solutions for aggressive behavior in dogs / by Pat Miller, CBCC-KA, CPDT-KA.
Description: Wenatchee, Washington : Dogwise Publishing, 2016. | Includes index.
Identifiers: LCCN 2016037936 | ISBN 9781617811937
Subjects: LCSH: Dogs--Behavior. | Aggressive behavior in animals. | Dogs--Training.
Classification: LCC SF433 .M567 2016 | DDC 636.7/0835--dc23
LC record available at https://lccn.loc.gov/2016037936

ISBN: 9781617811937

Printed in the U.S.A.

More praise for *Beware of the Dog*

Pat Miller has written an ideal response to a culture that has become sensitized to problems of dog aggression. She provides a detailed critique of the futility and inhumaneness of strong-armed dominance tactics and gives the reader sound antidotes in the form of scientific and effective approaches that enhance the communication between people and dogs.
Randall Lockwood, Ph.D. Senior Vice President, ASPCA

Pat Miller has given us the ultimate positive blueprint for helping dogs with aggression. She dispels the common myths about aggression, provides guidance for navigating what can be a frightening world for many of our pets and helps to bring peace back to families living with aggression. This is Pat Miller at her finest!
Dr. Lynn Honeckman, Veterinary Behavior Solutions, Orlando, FL.

Dedication

This book is dedicated to all the dogs out there who are struggling to make a confusing and scary world work for them in the only way they know how, and to all the humans working to make their world better. And to Nancy Kerns and *The Whole Dog Journal* for giving me a terrific platform all these years, and Kim Kilmer, who started all this many years ago when she was acquisitions editor for a publishing company by contacting me one day out of the blue after reading my *Whole Dog Journal* articles and asking, "Have you ever thought about writing a book…?" And finally and forever, to my wonderful husband, Paul, who always makes *my* confusing and scary world better.

Also to Dubhy, our sadly missed Scottie, who taught me all about living with a dog-reactive dog.

Table of Contents

ACKNOWLEDGMENTS

I can never in a million years thank Dr. Karen Overall enough for being a leader (and a goddess) in the field of force-free training, behavior and veterinary medicine, as well as for her support for my own work. A huge thanks also to training and behavior professionals and friends Beth Brock, PMCT3; Laura Dorfman, CPDT-KA, PMCT; Kelly Fahey, PMCT2; and Beth Joy, CPDT-KA, PMCT, for agreeing to review this manuscript. Your observations and comments were decidedly instrumental in making the book better. And, of course, to Dogwise, for providing an author-friendly platform for publication of excellent dog books that might otherwise never see the light of day.

Introduction

A good three-quarters of the clients in my canine behavior practice are seeing me because of their dogs' aggressive behaviors. The vast majority of the time, when the human is committed to implementing the management and modification protocols presented in this book, the dogs are successful at learning how to live in their world without resorting to aggression.

What do I mean by the terms management and modification? **Management** is the process of arranging a dog's environment to prevent opportunity for aggressive behavior to occur. If you are having guests over, put your fear-aggressive dog safely away in a back bedroom, give him a well-stuffed KONG and other chew toys to keep him happily engaged, and lock the door. **Behavior modification** is more complex. It means changing the dog's behavioral and emotional responses to stimuli that cause aggression so the dog no longer feels the need to aggress. It can involve changing a dog's association with an aggression-causing stimulus by pairing it with high-value treats ("Wow—scary men with beards make chicken happen—I think I'm starting to like men with beards!") or teaching a dog an alternative behavior to replace aggressive behaviors that he has learned. A dog who barks aggressively when visitors knock at the door can learn that a knock is his cue to run happily to his crate and wait for treats.

There are several important things I consistently tell my clients as they work with their dogs:

- There is no magic wand. Your dog's behavior will only change if you invest the time and effort into making it happen.
- Behavior modification is not linear. Don't despair if you seem to be making progress and then experience an apparent backslide. Keep working—it will get better.

- If you think you are going too slowly...slow down. Behavior modification takes time—if you rush it you will likely make things worse. Make haste slowly.
- Management is critically important to a successful modification program. You must create an environment where your dog isn't allowed and doesn't feel compelled to bite someone. Dogs who bite people tend to have short lives.
- If anything in your management/modification protocol seems to be making your dog's behavior worse instead of better, *stop* doing it, figure out what's going wrong and make necessary changes. (Of course I tell my clients to contact me immediately so I can help them make changes to the program.)

This book is intended to give the reader a better understanding of canine aggression, what it is and what causes it, along with science-based, force-free protocols for successful management and modification of aggression. Section One explains aggression, looks at our culture's perspective on aggression and debunks some of the myths about our dogs' aggressive behaviors. Section Two lays a foundation for managing and modifying aggressive behavior, whether you are a dog owner working with your own dog or a professional working with clients' dogs. Section Three discusses various presentations of aggression and offers protocols for working with them. Key terms are bolded when first used and are also defined in the Glossary beginning on page 182.

This book is written for owners who want to learn more about dog aggression and how to deal with it. However it is not intended to take the place of the services of a behavior professional if you find you need additional help. If your dog has a history of serious aggression, if you are afraid of your dog, and/or if you are doing appropriate work with him on your own and not making progress, please seek the assistance of a qualified, force-free behavior professional (see Chapter 18).

Canine aggression can be heartbreaking—when someone is injured, when the bond between the dog and his human is damaged or broken, and especially when the potential outcome is euthanasia for the biting dog. It is my fervent hope that this book will help you avoid that heartbreak.

SECTION I

Thoughts on Aggression

In this section we take a look at our culture's understanding of and relationship with canine aggression. What is aggression? How common is it, and how dangerous? Why do dogs growl, snarl, snap and bite? What causes a dog to appear perfectly fine with a person one day, and bite that same person the next day? It's not as mysterious as it sometimes seems.

CHAPTER 1

Aggression: What It Is; What It Isn't

In 1996, when my business, Peaceable Paws, was just a fledgling startup, the Monks of New Skete were still the rage, with their **"alpha roll"** (flipping a dog on his back and pinning him down until he stops struggling) approach to just about every canine misbehavior in the book. Positive reinforcement-based training was a brand new kid on the block, and despite my history of success with old-fashioned coercive training techniques for the competitive obedience arena, I embraced the new paradigm with open arms after my beloved dog Josie one morning hid from me under the back deck when I set out her training equipment. Alpha rolls and choke chains were out, clickers and treats were in.

I didn't start Peaceable Paws with the specific intention of handling aggression cases, but the cases came to me. With a paucity of qualified behavior professionals in my area (then Monterey/Santa Cruz) willing to work with dogs who exhibited aggressive behaviors, I decided I'd better become qualified. While I worked to educate myself on the intricacies of canine aggression, I hesitantly accepted a case or two, warning my clients that I may need to refer them (to whom, I wasn't sure) if I felt their dog's challenges were beyond my capabilities.

My first aggression case was a twelve-week-old Golden Retriever pup whose humans were first-time dog owners. Confounded by Teddie's puppy mouthing, they sought advice from their vet, who told them to alpha roll their pup. (Note: most veterinarians are not required to take a single course on behavior in college or in vet school, and many of them don't.) Not surprisingly, their pup's behavior was getting worse. Instead of innocent puppy mouthing—a normal behavior for a baby dog exploring the world—Teddie, perplexed and frightened by the sudden display of aggression from his previously kind and loving humans, was now biting defensively.

I realized this was a case I could handle. Just stop tormenting the pup and start training him and we're well on the road to recovery.

Clicks and treats, far superior to alpha rolls. Look at the trust and joy in both of these faces!

Not all my cases have been that easy, but the vast majority have stemmed from the same cause—a tragic misunderstanding of canine behavior, and an intense and hugely inappropriate human overreaction to what is often normal dog behavior. This behavior is, in most cases, simply a dog trying to cope with the complex, confusing and sometimes terrifying human world he lives in.

Fortunately, most of my clients, even those who may have used inappropriate methods in the past to try to stop their dogs' aggression, are relieved and delighted to hear that they don't need to be—in fact they *shouldn't* be—confrontational with their dogs. As **positive reinforcement training** (training that reinforces appropriate/desired behavior and does not use force, coercion or fear to extinguish unwanted behavior) has gained in popularity over the past two decades, increasingly we get phone calls from dog owners *seeking out* a behavior and training professional who won't exhort them to hurt and intimidate their dogs. That's exciting. Most dog owners really don't *want* to hurt their dogs, and are talked into doing so only because they want to believe that the service providers they are paying really do know what they are doing. Would that it were so.

As the pendulum swings encouragingly toward the positive side, it also swings back. The popularity of a genre of old-fashioned force-based television trainers spawned a whole new generation of alpha rollers, collar shockers and others investing time and energy into developing new ways to force dogs into submission.

As recently as a couple of years ago we got a phone call from a distraught dog owner. "Please don't tell me I have to kill my puppy!" she sobbed into the phone. Both her veterinarian and a local dog trainer (referred by the vet) had told her to alpha roll her twelve-week-old Rottweiler puppy for mouthiness, and when Helga became increasingly aggressive in response to the mistreatment, both advised her to euthanize the baby dog.

With a strong sense of déjà vu, I told her to stop the alpha rolling and start **clicker training** (positive reinforcement training that uses a marker signal, a clicker, to tell the dog when he has performed a behavior that earns a treat). Helga joined our puppy class, was a star student (just like Teddie), and now, all grown up, is a model canine citizen for her proud humans.

How common is dog aggression and how serious is it?

Aggression. It's a natural, normal dog behavior, but it's also a scary word that evokes images of maulings, and worse, dog-related fatalities. The term actually covers a long continuum of behaviors, some of them very appropriate and critically important to successful canine communication. This broad spectrum of behaviors is technically called **agonistic behavior.** So, while a growl-lunge-bite sequence would be easily recognized by most people as part of the aggression spectrum, subtler agonistic behaviors—such as a freeze, a hard stare or even avoidance behaviors like a retreat or a lack of eye contact—may not.

Aggression is probably the most common behavioral problem in dogs seen by behavior professionals and the most dangerous one seen in companion dogs. While the number of dog-related fatalities (approximately 35 per year in the U.S. Source: www.dogsbite.org/dog-bite-statistics-fatalities.php) pales in comparison to accidental death by other means, the number of annual reported bites is staggering. According to the *Dog Bite Law* website (www.dogbitelaw.com): *"The most recent official survey, conducted more than a decade ago, determined there were 4.7 million dog bite victims annually in the USA. A more recent study showed that 1,000 Americans per day are treated in emergency rooms as a result of dog bites. Dog bite losses exceed $1 billion per year, with over $300 million paid by homeowners insurance."*

Dog-related fatalities compared to other causes of human deaths

Based on various sources, estimated average annual U.S. human deaths caused by the following events are:

- Car—42,000
- Flu—20,000
- Murder—15,500
- Airline crashes—120
- Lightning—90
- Dog—35

Our culture and aggression

Our culture has become overly sensitized to dog bites. Once upon a time if Johnny was bitten by a neighbor's dog, Mom asked Johnny what he was doing to the dog that he shouldn't. Today she reaches for the phone to call her attorney. Once upon a time if the family dog snapped at the baby, Mom learned to be more careful about not letting the baby pull the dog's ears. Today she's dialing up a behavior professional, or worse, dropping the dog off at her local shelter. Sensationalized "dog mauls baby" headlines have turned us into a nation of aggress-a-phobes, where the smallest indication of discomfort on a dog's part sends humans screaming for their lawyers.

Behavior professionals mull over the causes of what looks to be a huge and growing problem. The population shift away from rural living and toward urban and suburban homes may have lessened our population's understanding of animal behavior in general. This lack of understanding manifests as inappropriate human behavior toward dogs, which triggers more aggressive behavior as well as a lower tolerance for bites—even minor ones. This same shift away from rural living has given dogs a much less stimulating lifestyle. Instead of following Farmer Bob around all day, herding livestock and helping with chores, today's dog is likely to spend the day sleeping, waiting for his human to come home from work. If he's lucky he gets a 15-minute walk when his owner gets home, then spends the evening hanging out with his couch-potato TV-watching human. If he seeks more mental or physical stimulation on his own, he's likely perceived as having behavior problems, when he's really just bored to tears.

A more responsible dog-owning population is keeping dogs at home rather than letting them wander freely as they did a few decades ago. That's a good thing, but as a result dogs may be less well-socialized—and more likely to bite. There has been an increase in popularity of dog breeds that contributes to our cultural sensitization—large, powerful breeds who can do serious damage if they bite, such as Pit Bulls and Rottweilers—as well as space-sensitive breeds who have a lower tolerance for inappropriate human behavior, such as Border Collies and Australian Shepherds. Finally, the appropriately diligent efforts of animal control authorities to quarantine dogs who bite (for rabies control purposes) and craft dangerous dog laws (for public safety purposes) have probably fueled the alarmist reactions to even minor dog bites.

I'm not saying that canine aggression isn't a serious issue. It's no fun when your dog bites. If he bites *you*, there can be a serious breach of trust, and the all-important bond that keeps the dog in his forever home for life can be damaged, sometimes beyond repair. If he bites your child there is legitimate concern for that young person's safety, guilt about having put your child at risk and the specter of Child Protective Services hovering over your shoulder. If he bites someone outside the family there is appropriate concern for that person's well-being, as well as fear of lawsuits and Animal Control consequences. And certainly, dogs have the potential to kill. (*www.dogsbite.org/dog-bite-statistics-fatalities.php*) Tragic.

Still, our culture is overly sensitized to dog bites and canine agonistic behavior (any behavior that could be perceived as threat, attack, appeasement or retreat, toward human or nonhuman members of the dog's social group). We need a new paradigm surrounding canine aggression. We need to understand that most of the social signals associated with aggression are normal and appropriate, not pathological, and that just because your dog growls at you when you approach while he's chewing a bone doesn't mean you're going to be the next mauling victim. In fact, most of the social signals associated with aggression are a dog's desperate attempt to *avoid* having to bite someone. It is when that someone misreads the signals and/or responds inappropriately that the dog is compelled to bite.

Short list of behaviors seen during agonistic encounters in dogs

- Avoidance
- Bared teeth (snarling)
- Biting*
- Body shake (shake off)
- Chasing
- Crouching
- Ears back
- Ears forward
- Excitement bark
- Frustration bark

- Warning growl
- Lick lips
- Look away
- Pawing
- Pilo-erection (hackles up)
- Play bow
- Play growl
- Prance
- Relaxed gaze into face
- Rolling on back
- Running away
- Sitting
- Snapping teeth
- Stalk
- Stare
- Submissive grin
- Tail wag
- Tail high (flag tail)
- Tail between legs
- Trembling
- Whine
- Yelping and showing teeth

*Note that biting is only one of 32 behaviors on this list

You may need to change your behavior!

While working with aggression cases over the years I've come to the realization that in many cases it's a far better tactic to change the human's behavior than the dog's. In fact, often, if we can just give the owner a different perspective and help her to stop overreacting to her dog's behavior, we can be successful in ending the aggression, even if we never change the dog's behavior at all. A growl, a snarl, a snap—these are all cries for help from a dog. If, instead of taking umbrage and aggressing back, we can empathize with the dog and try to understand what has made him so uncomfortable that he felt the need to communicate in this manner, then we have taken a giant step toward modifying the behavior.

When I do this...

You might remember the old joke: Man goes into his doctor's office and says, "Doc, when I do this it hurts." Doctor says, "Then stop doing that. That'll be $300."

I tell my clients that same joke—and relate it to their dog's aggression: They say, "When I do this my dog bites." I say, "Then stop doing that." They laugh, but I am dead serious. The first step in modifying canine aggression is to stop doing whatever it is that causes your dog to aggress.

Chapter 2

The Gift of Growl

My clients always appear a bit stunned at first when I tell them their dog's growl is a good thing. In fact, a growl is something to be greatly treasured. These are my aggression consult clients, who are in my office in desperation, often as a last resort, hoping to find some magic pill that will turn their biting dog into a safe companion. They are dismayed and alarmed to discover that the paradigm many of us grew up with—punish your dog harshly at the first sign of aggression—has only contributed to and exacerbated the serious and dangerous behavior problem that has led them to my door.

On one hand it seems intuitive to punish growling. Growling leads to biting, and dogs who bite people often must be euthanized, so let's save our dog's life and nip biting in the bud by punishing him at the first sign of inappropriate behavior. Makes sense, in a way, but when you have a deeper understanding of canine aggression, it's easy to understand why it's the absolute wrong thing to do.

Most dogs don't want to bite or fight. The behaviors that signal pending aggression are intended first and foremost to warn away a threat. The dog who *doesn't want to* bite or fight tries his hardest to make you go away. He may begin with subtle signs of discomfort that are often overlooked by many humans: tension in body movements, a stiffly-wagging tail, looking away, rolling onto his back. (Many people perceive a dog rolling onto his back as an invitation to be petted. This is sometimes the case—but not always. It can be an avoidance signal; the dog is asking you to go away.)

"Please," he says gently, "I don't want you to be here."

If you continue to invade his comfort zone, his threats may intensify, with more tension, a hard stare, maybe a little lip lift and a low growl.

"I mean it," he says more firmly, "I want you to leave."

If those are ignored, he may become more insistent, with an air snap, a bump of the nose or even open-mouth contact that closes gently on an arm but doesn't break skin.

"Please," he says, "don't *make* me bite you."

If that doesn't succeed in convincing you to leave, the dog may feel compelled to bite hard enough to break skin in his efforts to protect self, territory, members of his social group or other valuable resources.

What many people don't realize is that aggression is caused by stress. The stressor may be related to pain, fear, intrusion, threats to resources and past association or anticipation of any of these things. An assertive, aggressive dog attacks because he's stressed by the intrusion of another dog or human into his territory. A fearful dog bites because he's stressed by the approach of a human. An injured dog lacerates the hand of his rescuer because he's stressed by pain. A mother dog bites because she's stressed by the perceived threat to her puppies.

When you punish a growl or other early warning signs, you may succeed in suppressing the growl, snarl, snap or other warning behavior—but you don't take away the stress that caused the growl in the first place. In fact, you *increase* the stress, because now you, the dog's owner, have become unpredictable and violent as well. And if you succeed in suppressing the warning signs, you end up with a dog who bites without warning. He learns that it's not safe to warn.

Treasure your dog's warning signals. As alarming as this looks, he's trying his hardest not to bite you!

If a dog is frightened of children, he may growl when a child approaches. You, conscientious and responsible owner, are well aware of the stigma—and fate—of dogs who bite children, so you punish your dog with a yank on the leash and a loud "No! Bad dog!" Every time your dog growls at a child you do this, and quickly your dog's fear of children is confirmed—children do make bad things happen! He likes children even less ("children make my human angry!"), but he learns not to growl at them to avoid making you turn mean.

You think he's learned that it's not okay to be aggressive to children, because the next time one passes by, there's no growl.

"Phew," you think to yourself. "We dodged *that* bullet!"

Convinced that your dog now accepts children because he no longer growls at them, the next time one approaches and asks if he can pat your dog, you say yes. In fact, your dog has simply learned not to growl, but children still make him very uncomfortable. Your dog is now super-stressed, trying to control his growl as the child gets nearer and nearer so you don't get mean, but when the scary child reaches out for him he can't hold back any longer—he lunges forward and snaps at the child's face. Fortunately, you're able to restrain him with the leash so he doesn't connect. You, the dog, and the child are all quite shaken by the incident.

A growl is a dog's cry for help. It's your dog's way of telling you he can't tolerate a situation—as if he's saying, "I can't handle this, please get me out of here!"

Your first response when you hear your dog growl should be to calmly move him away from the situation (or move yourself away from him), while you make a mental note of what you think may have triggered the growl. Make a graceful exit. If you act stressed you'll only add to his stress and make a bite more, not less, likely. Don't worry that removing him rewards his growl—your first responsibility is to keep yourself and others safe and prevent your dog from biting.

If the growl was triggered by something *you* were doing, stop doing it. Yes, your dog learned one tiny lesson about how to make you stop doing something he doesn't like, but you'll override that when you do lots of lessons about how things that make him uncomfortable make *really, really good stuff* happen.

This is where a behavioral modification technique like **counter-conditioning and desensitization** (giving your dog a new association—usually giving him a positive association with something he dislikes or is afraid of, starting with a low intensity of stimulus and gradually working up to full intensity of stimulus) comes in. Your dog growls because he has a negative association with something—say he growls when you touch his paw. For some reason, he's convinced that having his paw touched is a bad thing. If you start by touching his knee or even farther up at his hip, then feeding him a smidgeon of chicken, and keep repeating that, he'll come to think that you touching his knee makes chicken happen. He'll want you to touch his leg so he gets a bit of chicken.

Note: Make sure your dog's discomfort with you touching his paw is not related to pain. If it hurts when you touch him there, counter-conditioning won't work until you eliminate the pain. It's a good idea to get a full veterinary workup to determine if your dog's growling and biting may be related to pain or some other medical condition.

When you see him eagerly search for chicken when you touch his knee, you can move your hand slightly lower and touch there, until you get the same "Where's my chicken?!" response at the new spot. Gradually move closer and closer to his paw, until he's delighted to have you touch his foot—it makes chicken happen! Now practice with each foot, until he's uniformly delighted to have you touch all of them. Remember that the touch comes first with each repetition, so it consistently predicts the imminent arrival of chicken.

Touch consistently predicts the imminent arrival of chicken.

If at any time in the process—which could take days, weeks or even months, depending on the dog, his degree of discomfort and how well you apply the protocol—you see the dog's tension increase, you've moved too quickly. Back up a few inches (or several!) to where he's comfortable being touched and start again. Or, there may be other stressors present that are increasing his tension. Do an environment check to be sure nothing else is happening that's adding to his stress. Have the rowdy grandkids leave the room, put the vacuum cleaner away, give him plenty of time to relax, and start again. "Plenty of time" could be anything from a few minutes to a half-hour or more, or even ending the session for the day and proceeding more carefully when you start up the next time.

Remember, dogs can't tell us in words what's bothering them, but they can communicate a lot with their body language and canine vocal sounds. Pay attention to what your dog is telling you. Listen with heart and compassion. Be gentle when your dog tells you he needs help. Come to his rescue. Treasure his growl.

CHAPTER 3

Listen With Your Eyes

"If only they could speak." Countless times I have heard a dog owner say that. And countless times I have swallowed my first retort: "But they *can* speak! You're just not listening..."

One of the most important keys to dealing with aggression is to be aware of what your dog is communicating. In the last chapter we discussed how the growl is actually a gift because it is a clear signal that the dog is uncomfortable. But there are other signals as well. You must become aware of what your dog is expressing. While the title of this book is "Beware of the Dog," it could just as well be "Be More Aware of Your Dog!"

We humans are a verbal species. We long for our beloved canine companions to speak to us in words we can easily understand. While they have some capacity for vocal communication, they'll never be able to deliver a soliloquy or carry on long, meaningful spoken conversations with their humans. English is a second language for them. Their first is body talk—body language communication in which they generally say, quite clearly, exactly what they mean. Our problem, and as a result theirs, is that we humans tend to listen with our ears, rather than our eyes, and miss much of what they are saying.

There are those who have spent a lot of time trying to understand dog behavior and have become skilled at reading canine body language. They seem to interact naturally with dogs, using their own subtle body language to communicate, as much as or more than they use words. But time alone doesn't grant this skill—there are also those who have spent a lot of time with dogs but are still woefully inept at properly interpreting the canine message.

The number of times a person has been bitten gives big clues as to his or her capacity to read, understand and properly respond to canine communications. No sane person wants to be bitten by a dog. If someone has been on the receiving end of canine teeth numerous times, either they aren't paying attention to what the dogs are saying, or they aren't responding appropriately. If a canine professional brags about how many times he's been bitten, run away fast—he clearly doesn't speak dog. Dogs almost always give clear—albeit sometimes subtle—signals before they bite. The mythical "bite without warning" is truly a rare occurrence. Most of the time the human just wasn't listening.

In their own words

Canine vocal communications can be classified as barks, growls, howls, whines and whimpers. Within those classifications, the sounds can have varying meanings. Your dog's voice must be taken in context with the rest of his behavior and body language for you to truly understand what he's saying to you.

Barking

Dogs bark for many reasons, including alert (there's something out there!), alarm (there's something bad out there), boredom, demand, fear, suspicion, distress and pleasure (play). The bark of a distressed dog, such as a dog who suffers from isolation or separation distress or anxiety, is high pitched and repetitive, getting higher in pitch as the dog becomes more upset. Boredom barking tends to be more of a repetitive monotone. An alert bark is likely to be a sharp, staccato sound; alarm barking adds a note of intensity to the alert.

Demand barks are sharp and persistent, and directed at the human who could/should ostensibly provide whatever the dog is demanding. At least, the dog thinks so. Suspicious barks are usually low in tone, and slow, while fearful barking is often low but faster. Play barking just sounds...playful. If you have any doubt—look to see what the dog is doing. If he's playing, it's probably play barking.

Growling

Growls are often a warning that serious aggression may ensue if you persist in whatever you're doing, or continue to expose him to whatever is stressing him in the environment. Rather than taking offense at your dog's growl, heed his warning, and figure out how to make him more comfortable with the situation. Dogs also growl in play. It's common for a dog to growl while playing tug—and that's perfectly appropriate as long as the rest of his body language says he's playing. If there's any doubt in your mind, take a break from play to let him calm down. Some dogs also growl in pleasure. Rottweilers, for example, are notorious for "grumbling" when being petted and playing, and absent any signs of stress, this is interpreted as a "feels good" happy sound.

Howling

Howling is often triggered by a high-pitched sound; many dogs howl at the sound of fire and police sirens. (Two of our own dogs howl when our donkey brays.) Some dog owners have taught their dogs to howl on cue—the owner howling or singing. Howling is generally considered to be communication between pack members, perhaps to locate another pack member or to call the pack for hunting. Some dogs howl when they are significantly distressed—again, a common symptom of isolation and separation distress.

Whining

Whining is a high-pitched vocalization, often produced nasally with the mouth closed. A dog may whine when he wants something, needs or wants to go outside, feels frustrated by leash restraint, is separated from a valued companion (human or otherwise), is excited or just wants attention. It is usually an indication of some increased level of stress for the dog.

Whimpering/Yelping

A whimper or a yelp is often an indication that a dog is in pain. This may happen when dogs play, if one dog bites the other dog too hard. The whimper or yelp is used to communicate distress to a canine pack member (or a human) with whom the dog is friendly. The other dog or human is expected to react in a way that shows they understand the communication. Whimpers can also indicate strong excitement, such as when an owner returns at the end of a long workday. Excitement whimpering is often accompanied by licking, jumping and barking. Whimpering is softer and less intense than whining.

Speaking words

Some dogs are capable of replicating human speech sounds. When these sounds are selectively reinforced, dogs can appear to be speaking human words, sometimes even sentences. It is most likely that the dogs have no concept of the meaning behind the words they are "speaking"—although as we learn more about canine cognition, one can't ever be too sure. It is interesting to note that one of the phrases most frequently taught to dogs by their owners is some version of "I love you..." YouTube provides some entertaining footage of talking dogs here: www.youtube.com/watch?v=bFsR772EByQ

Let me hear your body talk

The more you learn about your dog's subtle body language communications the better you'll be at reading them—and intervening appropriately, well before your dog is compelled to growl, snap or bite. It's important that you not focus on just one piece of the message. The various parts of your dog's body work together to tell the complete story, and unless you read them all and interpret them in context, you'll miss important elements of the equation. Be especially aware of the following body parts:

- **Tail**
- **Ears**
- **Eyes**

- **Mouth**
- **Hair**
- **Body posture**

Because dog communication is a constant flow of information, it's sometimes difficult to pick out small signals until you've become an educated observer. Start by studying photographs of dog body language, then watch videos that you can rewind and watch repeatedly, finally honing your skills on live dogs. Dog parks, doggie daycare centers and training class playgroups are ideal places to practice your observation skills. *The Language of Dogs* DVD set by Sarah Kalnajs, CPDT-KA, CDBC, is an excellent resource for body language study, as is Jill Breitner's *Dog Decoder* app at: www.dogdecoder.com.

A canine body parts dictionary

Despite conventional wisdom, a wagging tail doesn't always mean a happy dog. The following abridged Canine/English dictionary will help you become a skilled translator. Remember that breed characteristics can complicate the message. Relaxed ears and tail for an Akita (prick-eared, tail curled over the back) look very different from relaxed ears and tail for a Golden Retriever (drop-eared, long, low tail). Note that if body language vacillates back and forth it can indicate ambivalence or conflict, which may precede a choice toward aggression.

1. Tail

Tucked under: Submissive/appeasing, deferent or fearful

Low and still: Calm, relaxed

Low to medium carriage, gently waving: Relaxed, friendly

Low to medium carriage, fast wag: Submissive/appeasing or happy, friendly

High carriage, still/vibrating or fast wag: Tension, arousal, excitement; could be play arousal or aggression arousal

Circle wag: Happy, friendly

This dog is alert but not highly aroused. He is leaning forward, but his tail is relaxed, ears are to the side and his mouth is open and relaxed.

2. Ears

Pinned back: Submissive/appeasing, deference or fearful

Back and relaxed: Calm, relaxed, friendly

Forward and relaxed: Aware, friendly

Pricked forward: Alert, excitement, arousal, assertive; could be play arousal or aggression arousal

This dog is stressed. His ears are pinned back, his mouth is closed, there are stress lines over his eyes, and his forehead is wrinkled.

This dog is relaxed. His ears are forward but not pricked hard forward, his eyes are soft and his mouth is open and relaxed.

This dog is happy and relaxed. His ears are forward but not pricked hard forward, his mouth is open and smiling, and his eyes are squinty.

3. Eyes

Averted, no eye contact: Submissive/appeasing, deference or fearful; may be a subtle flick of the eyes, or may turn entire head away

Squinting, or eyes closed: Submissive/appeasing, happy greeting

Soft, direct eye contact: Calm, relaxed, friendly

Eyes open wide: Confident, assertive

Hard stare: Alert, excitement, arousal; could be play arousal or aggression

4. Mouth

Lips pulled back in a "V" shape: Submissive/appeasing or fearful (may also be lifted in "submissive grin" or "aggressive grin")

Licking lips, yawning: Stressed, fearful (or tired!)

Lips relaxed: Calm, relaxed, friendly

Lips puckered forward in a "C" shape, may be lifted (snarl): Assertive, threat

This dog is fearful. His ears are pinned back, his eyes are hard, he is behind the vertical (his hindquarters are lower than his shoulders) with a lowered body posture, and his lips are pulled back in a "V" shape. He is barking defensively to try to keep the threat from coming closer.

5. Hair

Piloerection or "raised hackles": Simply a sign of arousal. While it can indicate aggression, dogs may also piloerect when they are fearful, uncertain or engaged in excited play.

6. Body posture

Behind vertical, lowered; hackles may be raised: Submissive/appeasing or fearful

Vertical, full height: Confident, relaxed

Ahead of vertical, standing tall; hackles may be raised: Assertive, alert, excitement, arousal, possibly play arousal or aggressive arousal

Shoulders lowered, hindquarters elevated: A play bow—clear invitation to play; dog sending a message that behavior that might otherwise look like aggression is intended in play.

This dog is relaxed. His eyes are soft, his ears are hanging against the side of his head, and his mouth is open and relaxed.

This dog is somewhat aroused and/or excited. He is leaning forward (ahead of vertical), his tail is partly raised, his ears are forward and his eyes are intently focused. His mouth, however, is open and relaxed.

Be aware that some body language signals will occur in aroused play that look very similar to those that occur in conflict. Snarling, growling, even inhibited biting are common behaviors in canine play. If both dogs seem to be enjoying the interaction and keep coming back for more, it's probably play. If one of the dogs appears stressed, fearful and/or is trying to avoid interaction, then it may just be that the play is getting too rough for his comfort level, or it may be aggression rather than play. If you aren't confident about your ability to distinguish between appropriate play, inappropriate play and real aggression, ask your qualified positive behavior professional to help you.

Stress: Know it when you see it!

Dogs tell us when they are feeling stressed. The more aware you are of your dog's stress-related body language, the better you can help him out of situations that could otherwise escalate to inappropriate and dangerous behaviors. Many bites occur because owners fail to recognize and respond appropriately to their dogs' stress signals. Even aside from aggression, there are multiple reasons why it's important to pay attention to stress indicators:

- Stress is a universal underlying cause of aggression (see Chapter 5 for more details).
- Stress can have a negative impact on a dog's health.

- Dogs learn poorly when stressed.
- Dogs respond poorly to cues when stressed.
- Negative classical conditioning (see Chapter 8) can occur as a result of stress.

(Note that while we're discussing the above five reasons in relation to *canine* stress, they also apply to *all* species with a central nervous system—including humans…)

The smart, aware owner is always on the alert for signs that her dog is stressed, so she can alleviate tension when it occurs. Owners whose dogs are easily stressed often become hyper-vigilant, watching for tiny signs that presage more obvious stress-related behaviors, in order to forestall unpleasant reactions. If more owners were aware of these subtle signs of stress, fewer dogs would bite. That would be a very good thing.

Listed below are some stress behaviors that are often overlooked. With each behavior the appropriate immediate course of action is to identify the stressor(s) and determine how to decrease the intensity of that stressful stimulus. In many cases that's by increasing the distance between your dog and the stressor—be it a child, another dog, people in uniforms, men with beards, vacuum cleaners, garbage trucks, skateboards…

If possible, remove the stressor from your dog's environment entirely. If he's stressed by harsh verbal corrections, shock collars and warthogs, those are all things you can simply remove from his existence (unless you live in Africa, in which case warthog removal might prove challenging). For those stressors that can't be eliminated, a long-term program of counter-conditioning and desensitization can change your dog's association with a stressor from negative to positive, removing one more trigger for stress signals and possible aggression. Another strategy is to teach the dog a new **operant** (deliberate) response to the stressor—for example, teaching your dog that the sound of the doorbell means "Run to your crate to get a high-value treat."

Stress dictionary

Anorexia: Stress causes the appetite to shut down. A dog who won't eat moderate- to high-value treats may just be distracted or simply not hungry, but refusal to eat is a common indicator of stress.

Appeasement/Deference Signals: Appeasement and deference aren't always an indicator of stress. They are important everyday communication tools for keeping peace in social hierarchies, and are often presented in calm, stress-free interactions as a way of saying "I'm not challenging you." They are offered in a social interaction to promote the tranquility of the group and the safety of the group's members. When offered in conjunction with other behaviors, they can be an indicator of stress as well. Appeasement and deference signals include:

- Slow movement: appeasing/deferent dog appears to be moving in slow motion
- Lip licking: appeasing/deferent dog licks at the mouth of the higher-ranking member of the social group

- Sitting/lying down/exposing underside: appeasing/deferent dog lowers body posture, exposing vulnerable parts
- Turning head away, averting eyes: appeasing/deferent dog avoids eye contact, exposes neck
- Squatting and urinating

Avoidance: Dog turns away; shuts down; evades handler's touch and treats.

Brow Ridges: Furrows or muscle ridges in the dog's forehead and around the eyes.

Difficulty Learning: Dogs (and other organisms) are unable to learn well or easily when under significant stress.

Digestive Disturbances: Vomiting and diarrhea can be a sign of illness—or of stress; the digestive system reacts strongly to stress. Carsickness is often a stress reaction.

Displacement Behaviors: These are behaviors performed in an effort to resolve an internal stress conflict for the dog. They may be observed in a dog who is stressed and in isolation—for example a dog left alone in an exam room in a veterinary hospital—differentiating these behaviors from behaviors related to relationship communications.

- Blinking—eyes blink at a faster-than-normal rate
- Nose licking—dog's tongue flicks out once or multiple times
- Chattering teeth
- Scratching
- Shaking off (as if wet, but dog is dry)
- Yawning

Drooling: May be an indication of stress—or response to the presence of food, an indication of a mouth injury or a sign of digestive distress.

Excessive Grooming: Dog may lick or chew paws, legs, flank, tail and genital areas, even to the point of self-mutilation.

Hyperactivity: Frantic behavior, pacing, sometimes misinterpreted as "fooling around," ignoring or "blowing off" owner.

Immune System Disorders: Long-term stress weakens the immune system. Dogs with immune-related problems can benefit from lowering overall levels of stress.

Lack of Attention/Focus: The brain has difficulty processing information when stressed.

Leaning/Clinging: The stressed dog seeks contact with human as reassurance.

Lowered Body Posture: "Slinking," acting "guilty" or "sneaky" (all misinterpretations of dog body language) can be indicators of stress.

Mouthing: Willingness to use mouth on human skin—can be puppy exploration or adult poor manners, but can also be an expression of stress, ranging from gentle nibbling (flea biting) to hard taking of treats to painfully hard mouthing, snapping or biting.

Obsessive-Compulsive Disorders (OCDs): These include compulsive imaginary fly-snapping behavior, light and shadow chasing, tail chasing, pica (eating non-food objects), flank-sucking, self-mutilation and more. While OCDs probably have a strong genetic component, the behavior itself is usually triggered by stress.

Panting: Rapid shallow or heavy breathing—normal if the dog is warm or has been exercising, otherwise can be stress-related. Stress may be external (environment) or internal (pain, other medical issues).

Smiling: Sometimes described as the "submissive grin." Lips pull back from upper teeth—can be mistaken for a snarl, but is accompanied by other appeasing body language (i.e., ears back, squinty eyes) rather than offensive body language.

Stretching: To relax stress-related tension in muscles. May also occur as a non-stress behavior after sleeping or staying in one place for extended period.

Stiff Movement: Tension can cause a noticeable stiffness in leg, body and tail movements.

Sweaty Paws: Damp footprints can be seen on floors, exam tables, rubber mats.

Trembling: May be due to stress—or cold.

Whale Eye: White sclera of the dog's eye is visible around iris. May be due to stress and part of an agonistic warning, or may simply be that the dog's nose is pointed a different direction from his eyes.

Whining: High-pitched vocalization, irritating to most humans; an indication of stress. While some may interpret it as excitement, a dog who's excited to the point of whining is also stressed.

Yawning: Your dog may yawn because he's tired—or as an appeasement signal or displacement behavior.

Happy talk

We tend to focus on aggression signals because they are the most impressive and can predict danger. But any aware dog owner knows that dogs offer a lot of happy communications as well. Behaviors such as jumping up, pawing, nudging, barking and mouthing are often about happy excitement and attention-getting. Look for the signals that tell you your dog loves your new boyfriend, adores playing with the neighbor's kids, enjoys riding in the car, is happy to romp with your brother's dogs and totally digs chasing the tennis ball. It's important to pay attention to those communications as well so you know what makes him happy.

Your dog is speaking to you all the time. Remember to listen with your eyes.

CHAPTER 4

Alpha Schmalpha

The alpha myth is everywhere. Google "alpha, dog" and you get more than 85 million hits. Really. While not all the sites are about dominating your dog, there are literally millions of resources out there—websites, books, blogs, television shows, veterinarians, trainers and behavior professionals—instructing you to use force and intimidation to overpower your dog into submission. They say that you, the human, must be the alpha. They're all wrong. Every single one of them.

A history of dominance theory

The erroneous approach to canine social behavior known as **dominance theory** (two million-plus Google hits) is based on a study of captive zoo wolves conducted in the 1930s and 1940s by Swiss animal behaviorist Rudolph Schenkel, in which the scientist concluded that wolves in a pack fight to gain dominance, and the winner is the alpha wolf. Schenkel's observations of captive wolf behavior were erroneously extrapolated to wild wolf behavior, and then to domestic dogs. It was postulated that wolves were in constant competition for higher rank in the hierarchy, and only the aggressive actions of the alpha male and female held the contenders in check. Other behaviorists following Schenkel's lead also studied captive wolves and confirmed his findings: groups of unrelated wolves brought together in artificial captive environments do, indeed, engage in often-violent and bloody social struggles.

The problem is, that's not *normal* wolf behavior. As David Mech stated in a study of *wild* wolves, "Attempting to apply information about the behavior of assemblages of unrelated captive wolves to the familial structure of natural packs has resulted in considerable confusion. Such an approach is analogous to trying to draw inferences about human family dynamics by studying humans in refugee camps. The concept of the alpha wolf as a 'top dog' ruling a group of similar-aged compatriots…is particularly misleading."

What we know now, thanks to Mech and others, is that in the wild, a wolf pack is a family, consisting of a mated pair and their offspring of the past one to three years. Occasionally two or three families may group together. As the offspring mature they disperse from the pack; the only long-term members of the group are the breeding pair. By contrast, in captivity unrelated wolves are forced to live together for many years, creating tension between mature adults that doesn't happen in a natural wild pack.

But that's all about wolves anyway, not dogs. How did it happen that dog owners and trainers started thinking all that information (and misinformation) about wolf behavior had anything to do with dogs and dog behavior? According to an article in the July 30, 2010, issue of *Time*, somewhere along the line the logic went something like this: "Dogs are descended from wolves. Wolves live in hierarchical packs in which the aggressive alpha male rules over everyone else. Therefore, humans need to dominate their pet dogs to get them to behave."

Cesar Millan, the darling of the dominance crowd, is only the latest in a long line of dominance-based trainers who advocate forceful techniques such as the alpha roll. Much of this style of training has roots in the military—which explains the emphasis on punishment. As far back as 1906, Colonel Konrad Most was using heavy-handed techniques to train dogs in the German army, then police and service dogs. He was joined by William Koehler after the end of World War II. Koehler also initially trained dogs for the military prior to his civilian dog-training career, and his writings advocated techniques that including hanging and helicoptering a dog into submission (into unconsciousness, if necessary). To stop a dog from digging, he suggested filling the hole with water and submerging the dog's head in the water-filled hole until he was nearly drowned. (Obviously *not* a technique I recommend!)

Fast-forward several years to 1978 and the emergence of the Monks of New Skete as the new model for dog training, asserting a philosophy that "understanding is the key to communication, compassion, and communion" with your dog. The Monks were considered cutting edge at the time, and were in fact responsible for the widespread popularization of the alpha-wolf roll-over (now shortened to the alpha roll), in a complete and utter misinterpretation of the submissive roll-over that is *voluntarily offered* by the less assertive dog, not forcibly commanded by the stronger one. They also advocated the frequent use of other physical punishments such as the **scruff shake** (grab both sides of the dogs face and shake, lifting the dog off the ground) and **cuffing** under the dog's chin with an open hand several times, hard enough to cause the dog to yelp.

A submissive roll-over, voluntarily offered by the less assertive dog as an appeasement gesture or deference behavior—is not aggressively forced by the more assertive dog.

Avoidance roll-over—sometimes mistaken by humans as an invitation to belly rub. Note the tongue-flick and whale eye that suggest this dog is not inviting more intimate contact.

Relaxed roll-over—this little dog is dead to the world after a long day at a shaping (training) workshop—belly up, totally relaxed.

And some dogs really do roll over as an invitation for a belly rub. Note the hind leg sprawl and relaxed, open mouth.

Even the Monks' most recent book (2007), while professing that "training dogs is about building a relationship that is based on respect and love and understanding" is still heavy on outdated, erroneous dominance theory. Immediately following their suggestion that "a kindly, gentle look tells the dog she is loved and accepted," they say

"But it is just as vital to communicate a stern reaction to bad behavior. A piercing, sustained stare into a dog's eyes tells her who's in charge; it establishes the proper hierarchy of dominance between person and pet." *(Author's note: It can also elicit a strong aggressive response if you choose the wrong dog as the subject for your piercing, sustained stare.)*

Despite the strong emergence of positive reinforcement–based training in the last 20 years, the Monks don't seem to have grasped that the "respect" part needs to go both ways for a truly compassionate communion with your dog. Perhaps one of these days...

Enter the clicker

Just when it seemed that dog training had completely stagnated in turn-of-the-century military-style dominance-theory training, marine mammal trainer Karen Pryor wrote her seminal book, *Don't Shoot the Dog.* Originally published in 1985, this small, unassuming volume was intended as a self-help book for human behavior, the author never dreaming that her modest book, paired with a small plastic device that made a clicking sound, would launch a massive paradigm shift in the world of dog training and behavior. But it did.

Forward progress was slow until 1993, when veterinary behaviorist Dr. Ian Dunbar founded the Association of Pet Dog Trainers (now the Association of Professional Dog Trainers). Dunbar's vision of a forum for trainer education and networking has developed into an organization that now boasts nearly 5,000 members worldwide. While membership in the APDT is not restricted to positive reinforcement–based trainers, included in its guiding principles is this statement: "We promote the use of reward-based training methods, thereby minimizing the use of aversive techniques." The establishment of this forum facilitated the rapid spread of information in the dog training world, enhanced by the creation of an online discussion list where members could compare notes and offer support for a scientific and dog-friendly approach to training.

Things were starting to look quite rosy for our dogs. The positive market absolutely mushroomed with books and videos from dozens of quality training and behavior professionals, including Jean Donaldson, Dr. Patricia McConnell, Dr. Karen Overall, Suzanne Hetts and others. With advances in positive training and an increasingly educated dog training profession embracing the science of behavior and learning and passing good information on to their clients, pain-causing, abusive methods such as the alpha roll, scruff shake, hanging, drowning and cuffing appeared to be headed the way of the passenger pigeon.

Then, in the fall of 2004, the National Geographic Channel launched its soon-to-be-wildly-popular show, *The Dog Whisperer,* over the protests of several degreed behavior professionals to whom they had sent a review clip several months earlier. Nat Geo was clearly informed in advance of that first airing that the star of the show, Cesar Millan, was using methods that were outdated, unscientific and potentially dangerous. "Don't do it," the experts warned. The show aired anyway. Dominance theory was back in vogue, with a vengeance. Today, everything from housetraining mistakes to jumping up to counter surfing to all forms of aggression is likely to be attributed to "dominance" by followers of the alpha-resurgence.

Why not alpha?

"But," some will argue, "look at all the dogs who have been successfully trained throughout the past century using the dominance model. Those trainers can't be *all* wrong."

In fact, harsh, force-based methods are a piece of operant conditioning (known as "positive punishment"), and as the decades have proven, those methods *can* work. They are especially good at **shutting down behaviors**—convincing a dog that it's not safe to do anything unless instructed to do something. And yes, that works with some dogs. With others, not so much.

My own personal, unscientific theory is that dog personalities lie on a continuum from very soft to very tough. Harsh, old-fashioned dominance-theory methods *can* effectively suppress behaviors without *obvious* fallout (although there is *always* behavioral fallout) with dogs nearest the center of the personality continuum—those who are resilient enough to withstand the punishment, but not so tough and assertive that they fight back. Under dominance theory, when a dog fights back, you must fight back harder until he submits, in order to assert yourself as the pack leader, or alpha. Problem is, sometimes they don't submit, and the level of violence escalates. Or they submit for the moment, but may erupt aggressively again the next time a human does something violent and inappropriate to them. Under dominance-theory training, those dogs are often deemed incorrigible, not suitable for the work they're being trained for nor safe as a family companion, and sentenced to death. Many of them, had they never been treated so inappropriately in the first place, might have been perfectly fine.

At the opposite end of the spectrum, a very soft dog can easily be psychologically damaged by one enthusiastic assertion of "rank" by the heavy-handed dominance trainer. This dog quickly shuts down, fearful and mistrusting of the humans in his world who are unpredictably and unfairly violent.

Most **crossover trainers** (those who originally trained using old-fashioned methods and now are proud to promote positive reinforcement–based training) will tell you they successfully trained lots of dogs the old way. They loved their dogs and their dogs loved them. I'm a crossover trainer, and I know that's true. I also know that I would dearly love to be able to go back and redo all of that training, to be able to have an even better relationship with those dogs, to give them a less stressful life, and one filled with even more joy than the one we shared together. Where's a DeLorean and a flux capacitor when you need one?

Finally, the very presumption that our dogs would even consider us humans to be members of their canine pack is simply ludicrous. They know how impossibly inept we are, for the most part, at reading and understanding the subtleties of canine body language. We are equally inept, if not even more so, at trying to mimic those subtleties. Any attempts on our part to somehow insert ourselves into their social structure and communicate meaningfully with them in this manner are simply doomed to failure. It's about time we gave up trying to be dogs in a dog pack and accepted that we are humans miraculously coexisting with another species—and that we're most successful doing so when we coexist peacefully.

The fact is, successful social groups work because of voluntary deference, *not* because of aggressively enforced dominance. The whole *point* of social body language rituals is to *avoid* conflict and confrontation, not to *cause* it. Watch any group of dogs interacting. Time and time again you'll see dogs deferring to each other. It's not even always the same dog deferring:

> Dog B: Hey, I'd really like to go first.
>
> Dog A: By all means, be my guest.
>
> Dog B passes down the narrow hallway.

> Dog A: I'd really like to have that bone.
>
> Dog B: Oh sure—I didn't feel like chewing right now anyway.
>
> Dog A gets the bone.

What we know now is that yes, social hierarchies do exist in groups of domesticated dogs, and in many other species, including humans. We also know that hierarchy can be fluid. As described above, one dog may be more assertive in one encounter, and more deferent in the next, depending on what's at stake, and how strongly each dog feels about the outcome. There is a myriad of subtleties about how those hierarchies work, and how the members of a social group communicate—in any species.

We also know that canine-human interactions are not driven by social rank, but rather by reinforcement. Behaviors that are reinforced repeat and strengthen. If your dog is doing an inappropriate behavior such as counter surfing or getting on the sofa, it's not because he's trying to take over the world—it's just because he's reinforced by finding food on the counter, or by being comfortable on the sofa. He's a scavenger and an opportunist, and the goods are there for the taking. Figure out how to prevent him from being reinforced for the behaviors you don't want, and reinforce him liberally for the ones you do, and you're well on your way to having the relationship of *mutual* love, respect, communication and communion that we all want to have with our dogs.

Comments and resources on "Alpha" dominance theory

There is a growing body of information available to anyone who wants to learn more about why dominance theory is so outdated and incorrect. Here are ten resources to get you started:

1. The American Society of Veterinary Animal Behaviorists Position Statement on Dominance (excerpt): "The AVSAB recommends that veterinarians not refer clients to trainers or behavior consultants who coach and advocate dominance hierarchy theory and the subsequent confrontational training that follows from it." *(www.avsab.org/resources/position-statements/)*

2. The Association of Professional Dog Trainers Position Statement on Dominance (excerpt): "The APDT's position is that physical or psychological intimidation hinders effective training and damages the relationship between humans and dogs. Dogs thrive in an environment that provides them with clear structure and communication regarding appropriate behaviors, and one in which their need for mental and physical stimulation is addressed. The APDT advocates training dogs with an emphasis on rewarding desired behaviors and discouraging undesirable behaviors using clear and consistent instructions and avoiding psychological and physical intimidation. Techniques that create a confrontational relationship between dogs and humans are outdated." *(www.apdt.com/about/ps/dominance.aspx)*

3. Certified Applied Animal Behaviorist Kathy Sdao (article excerpt): "But even if dogs did form linear packs, there's no evidence to suggest that they perceive humans as part of their species-specific ranking. In general, humans lack the capability to even recognize, let alone replicate, the elegant subtleties of canine body language. So it's hard to imagine that dogs could perceive us as pack members at all."

4. Patricia McConnell, PhD—ethologist (article excerpt): "People who argue that ethology supports 'getting dominance over your dog' are not only focused on an issue more relevant 50 years ago than today, they are misrepresenting the findings of early researchers on social hierarchy. Social hierarchies are complicated things that allow animals to live together and resolve conflicts without having to use force every time a conflict comes up." *(www.4pawsu.com/pmdominance.htm)*

5. Meghan Herron, DVM (article excerpt): "Our study demonstrated that many confrontational training methods, whether staring down dogs, striking them, or intimidating them with physical manipulation such as alpha rolls (holding dogs on their back), do little to correct improper behavior and can elicit aggressive responses." *(www.sciencedirect.com/science/article/pii/S0168159108003717)*

6. Sophia Yin, DVM (blog excerpt): "Experts say dominance-based dog-training techniques made popular by TV can contribute to bites." *(www.drsophiayin.com/blog/entry/experts_say_dominance-based_dog_training_techniques_made_popular_by_televis)*

7. Study, University of Bristol (article excerpt): "Far from being helpful, the academics say, training approaches aimed at 'dominance reduction' vary from being worthless in treatment to being actually dangerous and likely to make behaviours worse." (2009, May 21). Using 'Dominance' To Explain Dog Behavior Is Old Hat. Science Daily *(www.sciencedaily.com / releases/2009/05/090521112711.htm)*

8. Jean Donaldson, *The Culture Clash* (Dogwise Publishing) 2005: "The dominance panacea is so out of proportion that entire schools of training are based on the premise that if you can just exert adequate dominance over the dog, everything else will fall into place. Not only does it mean that incredible amounts of abuse are going to be perpetrated against any given dog, probably exacerbating problems like unreliable recalls and biting, but the real issues, like well-executed conditioning and the provision of an adequate environment, are going to go unaddressed, resulting in a still-untrained dog, perpetuating the pointless dominance program."

9. Barry Eaton, *Dominance in Dogs: Fact or Fiction* (Dogwise Publishing) 2011: "...the alpha wolf is not the dictator of a pack, but a benevolent leader, and domestic dogs are not dictatorial and are unlikely to try to raise their status to rule over other dogs in a pack environment." And "I believe it's time to open our minds and consider the concept of pack rules as a thing of the past and recognize that dogs are not constantly trying to dominate their owners."

10. James O'Heare, *Dominance Theory and Dogs* (Dogwise Publishing) 2008: "...while the notion of social dominance holds potential for value in a social psychology and ethology context, it is an insidious idea with regards to explaining and changing behavior between companion dogs or dogs and people...it should be abandoned completely in that context in favor of a more efficient, effective and scientifically defensible behavioral approach." And from an APDT interview with James O'Heare: "The most significant problem with viewing dog-human relationships in the context of social dominance is that it implies and promotes an adversarial relationship between the two. It sets up a win-lose scenario, that actually ends up in a lose-lose scenario (as most win-lose scenarios do). It is incompatible with cooperation by its very nature, cooperation being something you need to promote an effective bond and training environment."

CHAPTER 5

Stress, the Root Cause of Aggression

Across the board, with one tiny exception so rare it's barely worth mentioning, aggression is caused by stress. Whatever "classification" of aggression an owner or behavior professional chooses to use, the underlying cause of the aggression is stress. There is usually a *triggering* stressor—when a dog bites a child it's a good bet that child was a stressor for him—but there is also a background noise of other stressors that pushed the dog over his bite threshold with *that* child on *that* particular day. We call this **trigger stacking.** These are often stressors that we don't even notice, and because cortisol, an important stress hormone that plays a role in aggression, can stay in the system for at least two days, perhaps a lot longer, they can be stressors that occurred yesterday, or even the day before!

Think of it as canine road rage. In the human world, road rage might look like this:

- **Stressor #1:** Our subject jumps out of bed in the morning realizing that his alarm didn't go off and he's late for work.
- **Stressor #2:** He dashes through a cold shower because his hot water tank's on the blink.
- **Stressor #3:** As he hurries out the door his eye falls on the foreclosure notice that arrived in yesterday's mail because his mortgage payment is overdue.
- **Stressor #4:** He jumps in his car, starts the engine and sees that his gas gauge is on "E." He's already late and now he has to stop to fill up his tank.
- **Stressor #5:** As he pulls onto the freeway his cell phone dings to remind him of an important meeting in 15 minutes—and his commute is 25 minutes.
- **Stressor #6:** He remembers that his boss warned him that if he's late for one more important meeting he'll be fired. If he speeds, maybe he can make it.

- **Stressor #7:** Traffic is a little slow, but if he runs the commute lane, maybe he can make it. Just as he starts to pull into the left lane a car cuts him off and then pokes along in front of him below the speed limit. It's the last straw. Over threshold, he reaches under his seat pulls out his loaded .38 and...

In the dog world, canine road rage might look like this:

- **Stressor #1:** Dog has a little isolation distress, usually mitigated by the presence of his canine sibling, but today his brother got dropped off at the vet hospital when his humans went off to work, so he's all alone.
- **Stressor #2:** UPS delivery arrives, and dog has a "thing" about delivery people.
- **Stressor #3:** Just before noon a thunderstorm passes through. Dog is thunder sensitive, and owner didn't give him his thunder medication this morning.
- **Stressor #4:** Pet walker is supposed to arrive at 1:00 p.m., but is late and doesn't get there until 2:30. Dog is stressed by change in routine and by urgency of a very full bladder by the time the walker arrives.
- **Stressor #5:** Humans arrive home at their normal time but they are stressed because dinner guests are due at 7:00 p.m. and they have to get ready. Dog is stressed by his humans' stress, and the fact that they rush through *his* evening routine, feeding him hurriedly and skipping his walk to the dog park for exercise.
- **Stressor #6:** Visitors arrive, and while the dog is fine with adult visitors, he is not especially fond of children, and there are four in this family. All throughout dinner, the dog listens to the high-pitched sounds of children's voices laughing and arguing, and occasionally sees them staring at him.
- **Stressor #7:** After dinner the kids are running around the house. The dog tries to stay out of their way, but eventually one corners him in the kitchen. Over threshold, he pulls out his loaded mouth and...

Stress is an emotional and physiological response to a stimulus. The foundational underpinning of aggression is based on classical conditioning—your dog's emotional and physical response to a stimulus that causes him stress: fear, pain, anger and/or some other strong emotion. He can't help his emotional response any more than you can when faced with something that scares or hurts you. Aggression also has an operant piece—your dog learns that he can deliberately act to make scary stressors go away. When he growls, barks and lunges, perceived bad things tend to leave—so his aggressive behavior is **negatively reinforced** (dog's behavior makes a bad thing go away), and increases over time.

Aggression is *not* dominance

I know this was discussed in Chapter 4, but it is worth repeating here since behavior caused by stress is so often mistakenly viewed as some sort of dominance behavior. The concept of dominance in a social group has been so widely misunderstood and distorted that many knowledgeable behavior professionals hesitate to even use the term. In fact, dominance has little to do with aggression, and all to do with access to desired resources: the concept of dominance strictly refers to an interaction or a series of interactions between two individuals in which there is an outcome in favor of one member of the pair. That outcome is largely determined by a submissive or yielding response from one of the individuals and *not* through overt conflict or escalated aggression. Someone who is truly higher ranking in social status doesn't *need* to resort to aggression to get what he wants. This holds true for social groups of all species, including humans. Violent behavior between group members is inappropriate and unacceptable in social interactions. Violence is not a good survival strategy—especially in the wild, if a member of the social group is injured, that individual is likely to die.

Using violent behavior against a dog who is aggressive adds additional stress to his stress load. You may be able to suppress his aggressive behavior in that moment, but you have likely increased the probability for future, possibly more intense, aggression to occur. There are far more appropriate and effective ways to manage and modify aggressive behavior than aggressing back.

So what do you *do* when your dog exhibits aggressive behavior? Remember that stress, not any desire to take over the world, causes aggression to erupt. The first thing to do is educate yourself about dog body language so you can be aware of your dog's subtler agonistic behaviors. Then be aware of your dog's stressors and stress levels, and avoid putting him in situations where he may be compelled to bite. When you do see stress signals, even subtle ones, remove him from the immediate proximity of the stressor to help him cope with the situation.

Focus on reducing stress in your dog's life

When you've identified something that appears to be a stressor for him, figure out how to remove it as a stressor in his life. If it's something you can get rid of, simply get rid of it. If you can manage it, by removing him from the environment when you know the stressor will be present, do it. If it's too present in his world to get rid of or manage, take steps to change his opinion of that stressor through counter-conditioning, or change his behavior in the presence of that stressor through operant conditioning. Finally, there will be some low-level stressors that he'll just have to live with. As long as they aren't significant enough to put him near or over his bite threshold, he can live with some stressors. We *all* have *some* stress in our lives...

Here are some examples:

1. **Get rid of it:** Anything aversive that causes unnecessary pain or stress, including shock collars, choke chains and prong collars, penny cans or throw chains. Even head halters, considered by some professionals to be positive training tools, are aversive to many dogs.

2. **Manage it:** If your dog isn't fond of small children and there are *none* in your life and he doesn't encounter them regularly in your neighborhood, you can manage him the one time each year your sister comes to visit with your young niece and nephew, by keeping him in another part of the house when the kids are awake and about.

3. **Change his association:** Convince him that something that stresses him is actually very wonderful by pairing it consistently with something else wonderful. If your dog is stressed by men with beards, you can convince him that men with beards always make chicken happen, by having a bearded man appear, and feeding the dog bits of chicken, over and over and over again, until he *wants* furry-faced men to appear so he can have more chicken. The key to successful counter-conditioning, as this process is called, is to always keep the dog below threshold; you want him a little aware of and worried about the aversive stimulus, but not quaking in fear or barking and lunging (see Counter-conditioning, Chapter 8).

4. **Teach him a new behavior:** Perhaps your dog becomes highly aroused by visitors coming to the door. He's not fearful or aggressive, but the high arousal is a stressor. You can teach him that the doorbell is his cue to run and get in his crate, where he'll receive a stuffed KONG or other doggie delectable. Or you can teach him that visitors toss toys for him to chase if he sits politely when the door opens.

5. **Live with it:** So you're a little (or a lot!) stressed because your work isn't going well, or the school just notified you that your teenage daughter has been skipping school. Your stress can be a stressor for your dog! They are so good at reading our body language that the tension you exhibit when you are stressed will add to your dog's stress load. While I encourage you for your own well-being to take steps to reduce your stress as much as possible, this is one your dog may be able to live with, especially if you remember that when you are stressed, it pushes your dog a little closer to his own bite threshold—so it might not be a good time to do his counter-conditioning exercises.

When aggression happens

What if you misjudge a situation and something happens that puts your dog over threshold and causes him to display seriously aggressive behavior, perhaps even biting someone? First, don't panic. All dogs can bite, and the fact that yours has doesn't make him a Cujo. You will need to:

- Move him away from the scene. Stash him in another room, stick him in your car for a moment or hand his leash to someone he knows who is not at risk for being bitten, and have them take him away.

- Apologize. A good apology is, "Oh, I am so sorry you (or your dog, or your child) were bitten!"
- Examine the site of the bite. Take a couple of quick photos if you can. If the bite broke skin, offer first aid (if you have it). If the injuries are serious, call 9-1-1, or see that the victim has a way to access medical care.
- If it's clear that your dog was the sole offender, you may want to offer to pay for medical or veterinary care. A pre-emptive discussion with your attorney about this possibility is a good idea, to prevent yourself from taking on more liability than is appropriate, while still doing the ethical and reasonable thing. If it's unclear who "started it," be wary of immediately accepting responsibility for the incident.
- Prepare for a visit from animal control. These days, in most parts of the country, if a dog bite breaks human skin the dog must be quarantined for at least ten days. Have your current rabies certificate handy—they *will* ask to see it—a rabies tag isn't enough. In many jurisdictions you may be able to quarantine your dog in your own home. If not, find out if your dog can be kept at a vet hospital for the required period—it's usually a safer, less stressful place than a shelter. If animal control insists on taking your dog away for quarantine, *do not sign anything* until you have read it carefully and are sure you understand it. Some dog owners have unknowingly and tragically signed their dogs over for euthanasia when they thought they were just agreeing to quarantine.
- Prepare for dangerous dog proceedings. Depending on the laws in your area, your dog may be declared "potentially dangerous" for acting aggressively, or "dangerous" for actually biting someone. It's good to read your local ordinance now, even if your dog never bites anyone, and for sure *after* a bite happens. If your dog is designated dangerous or you do get called to a hearing of some kind in relation to your dog's aggressive behavior, you'd be wise to involve your attorney. There are now attorneys specializing in animal law, and as a general rule, they are your best choice for dangerous dog cases.

Prevention

Basic training and early socialization can go a long way toward inoculating your dog against future aggression (see Chapter 6 for more details). Your observational skills and ability to mitigate stressful situations for your dog are excellent booster shots. At that point, however, when you become aware that your dog's behaviors are inappropriate, traveling along that continuum of agonistic behavior verging on overt aggression, and are resistant to your efforts to manage and modify them, it's time to call for help.

Remember that a good behavior professional won't come riding in like a white knight, push your dog around a little and declare him cured. A good behavior modification protocol is not drama, and aggressive behavior isn't fixed in an hour. Your behavior professional should provide you with a slow, low-key program that will help your dog learn to cope with his world. She won't need to see the actual aggressive behavior—she will trust your description of your dog's reaction to the stressors in his world, and help you figure out how to keep him far below his bite threshold. Like most behaviors, aggression is far easier to modify sooner, before your dog has had time to practice and get good at it.

SECTION II

Working With Aggression

In this section we lay the foundation for your work with your (or a client's) aggressive dog, and create a framework—the outline of a general procedure to follow for a thorough and complete behavior modification program.

CHAPTER 6

Socialization

If you're reading this book, chances are good that for at least one of your dogs—or a dog you are working with—it's too late for prevention. Still, a book on aggression wouldn't be complete without a discussion of how to avoid behaviors that all too often end in the loss of a dog's life, after he has inflicted injury to humans or another animal.

The number one most important prescription to inoculate a dog against aggressive behavior is proper socialization. Running a very close second is being scrupulously careful about who you allow to interact with/handle your dog, and being adamant about how they do so. Let's start with **socialization**—helping your young dog learn that the world is a safe and happy place through careful exposure to all kinds of different people, places and things.

The social scene

In 2008, the American Veterinary Society for Animal Behavior (AVSAB) released a statement affirming that puppy socialization is a critically important tool in the development of a behaviorally normal dog. *(https://kathysantodogtraining.com/wp-content/uploads/KSDTAVSABPuppySocialization.pdf)*

They also confirmed that the risk of contracting a serious or fatal disease during proper puppy socialization efforts is *far* less a concern than the risk of a dog being given up or euthanized in the future due to behavior problems that developed as a result of a lack of socialization. One might think that when AVSAB makes a definitive statement on a behavior topic, the case would be closed. Apparently not.

It recently came to my attention that an internationally-known speaker and dog trainer is asserting that puppies don't have a prime socialization period, that they should remain with their litters until they are ten to twelve weeks old, and that puppy training classes are bad for puppies and should be avoided. I was floored. Sounds like the perfect recipe for creating an unsocialized (and fear-aggressive) dog! I also, in my behavior practice, still come across the occasional client whose veterinarian has exhorted them not to take their pup anywhere out in public until she is fully vaccinated, somewhere between the ages of four and six months. Not floored by this, but still disappointed. Not surprisingly, I'm usually seeing those clients' dogs for fear-related behaviors, often aggression, stemming from a lack of adequate socialization during puppyhood.

What is socialization?

Socialization involves introducing a puppy to a variety of stimuli (sights, sounds, smells, experiences) *and making sure the pup is having a good time while doing so.* Canine behavior scientists have determined that the "socialization window" is even smaller than once thought, now pretty much agreeing that the period only extends from three weeks to about 14 weeks instead of the previously-held 20 weeks. This is the critically important time for a pup to receive a good education about the world around her.

Note that this very important socialization period is half over by the time most pups go to their forever homes around the age of eight weeks. Let me repeat that. *Half over!* Breeders *must* do their share—if a puppy is already fearful at the age of eight weeks, super-socialization for the month that remains will help, but not ever completely make up for the missing time. Puppy buyers can easily lose their hearts to the shy puppy who hides under the chair, telling themselves that the little one just needs love to help overcome his fears. Unfortunately, this is usually *not* the case—these pups generally require a *lot* of behavior modification to become even *close* to normal.

If the puppy has a genetic predisposition for a confident personality, *some* of the damage can possibly be repaired, but it takes hard work in addition to love. Still, he will probably never be the confident, outgoing dog he *could* have been with better socialization during those first eight weeks.

Since behavior is *always* a combination of genetics and environment, if a pup is genetically predisposed to be timid, early socialization is even more critically important. Absent that, dog and human are probably in for ten to 15 years of significant behavior challenges. Given that fear is the most common cause of aggression, and that dogs who bite people tend to have short lives, pups who are not well-socialized and/or are not genetically predisposed to be confident may be looking at a dim future. Since much of the time we really have no knowledge of a pup's genetic predisposition for confident or timid personality, the answer is to super-socialize *every* pup we get our hands on.

Wherever your pup hails from (breeder, shelter, rescue, friend), *ask* detailed questions about the socialization he's had so far. How many different places has he been? How many different kinds of people has he met? What kinds of activities has he done? How did he react to all those things? Your pup should have already at least happily met the "ding!" of the microwave oven, sounds of the washer and dryer, ringing telephone, radio, television, grooming brush and nail clippers, and dozens of different/varied humans. If you're meeting him in a puppy pen, ask if you can take him outside, away from his littermates. Sometimes a pup will act normal in his familiar environment surrounded by family members whose presence gives him confidence, but become very fearful in a new place. *(Note—the good breeder will have already worked with him away from his mom and littermates so his rehoming separation is less of a shock to him.)* If you elect to purchase or adopt that timid puppy anyway, know that you are setting yourself up for *lots* of behavior work. Let me say that again. *Lots.*

Well-socialized puppies become optimists—believing that the world is a happy place and that new things they encounter are probably safe and good unless proven otherwise. They tend to be resilient—able to bounce back quickly in adulthood even if/when a traumatic event occurs. An unsocialized or under-socialized puppy becomes a pessimist. Everything new is scary and suspect unless you can convince him otherwise—and it's not easy to do that—hence the generally fearful nature of an under-socialized dog. Traumatic events only confirm his strongly held belief that the world is scary and dangerous.

Appropriate puppy socialization takes place during a well-run positive puppy training class.

How to socialize

Remember that socialization is giving your pup *good* experiences with new things, not just *exposing* him to new things. To the extent possible, control the environment. Introduce him to children who you know behave appropriately around dogs; don't just let him be mobbed by the entire Little League team. Socialize him with other dogs by enrolling in a well-run puppy class that allows puppy playtime as part of the curriculum. Don't take him to the dog park—it's too risky. If you want him to meet an adult dog, select a dog you know well, one who will be appropriate with him, and introduce them using an appropriate procedure. Walk him on suburban sidewalks before exposing him to big city streets. Give your mail carrier and your UPS delivery person high-value treats to feed him when they meet.

Pair your pup's exposure to new things with generous delivery of small (pea-sized) bits of very high-value treats, so he thinks new stuff means good stuff. If he's comfortable meeting new humans, give them several treats to give him, so "new humans" become reliable predictors of "yummy treats!" (Be sure to strongly caution your humans not to grab for or otherwise frighten him.) If he's a bit worried about new humans, *you* feed the high-value treats in the presence of strangers until he is quite happy about their presence, *then* they can feed him the treats.

You can also use favored activities—play with a toy, scratches behind the ear, searching on the ground for "Find It" treats (see Chapter 10 for more about "Find It")—to give him a positive association with new people, places and new things. Your socialization goal is to *always* make sure he is *always* having a good time as you introduce him to the world during this important period of his life.

Appropriate play between a puppy and an adult dog in the real world.

If he won't eat super-scrumptious treats or won't play with his favorite toy, he is telling you he is very uncomfortable with his surroundings. You need to act *immediately* by moving him away to a safe distance—far enough away that he's happy to take treats and play again. Make a mental note (and write it down later) of what it was that was of concern to him, and plan to do more work around that stimulus—be it a certain type of human (male, child, large, small, pushing a cart, wearing a uniform, etc.), a thing (garbage truck, elevator, manhole cover, another dog, recycle bin, etc.), a sound (thunder, beeping of a truck backing up, applause, crowd cheering) or a surface (gravel, cement, sand, hardwood floor). In each case, you will use counter-conditioning and desensitization (see Chapter 8) to work on increasing his comfort level, by presenting the thing (the stimulus) at an intensity he is comfortable with, and feeding treats or playing with toys there until he is happy. Increasing distance will usually decrease intensity. When you are far enough away you can use treats and/or toys to get him happy, then very gradually move closer—sometimes by inches at a time—and get him happy at each new location before moving closer again.

Puppy socialization with lots of different people in lots of different places.

Other experiences most pups should have at an early age include:

- **Places:** car, vet, beach, park, woods, trails, wildlife, school, shops, friends' houses, crate, public transport, grooming parlor (ask permission first), cafe, training facility (ask permission first), stairs, hardwood floors, carpet, gravel, grass, cement, other unusual surfaces (walking on a tarp, a teeter-totter, stone wall, fallen log)
- **People:** friends, neighbors, family, children, elderly people, men with deep voices, men with beards, people of different races, people in hats and sunglasses, people wearing various ethnic dress like saris or turbans, people carrying umbrellas and bags, wearing tool belts, wearing a backpack, people in uniform, people with wheelchairs, strollers or walkers, people on bicycles, people on skateboards, people running, people crawling, people playing sports, people who ignore dogs, people who are affectionate toward dogs

- **Animals:** other puppies, other dogs, individual dogs, groups of dogs, working dogs, playing dogs, cats, Guinea pigs, rabbits, parrots, poultry, horses, livestock
- **Things:** grooming brush, nail trimmer, crate, leash, broom, vacuum, dishwasher, fan, weed-whacker, power tools, ladder, children's toys, manhole covers, tractor, wagon, snow blower

You get the idea...the possibilities are endless!

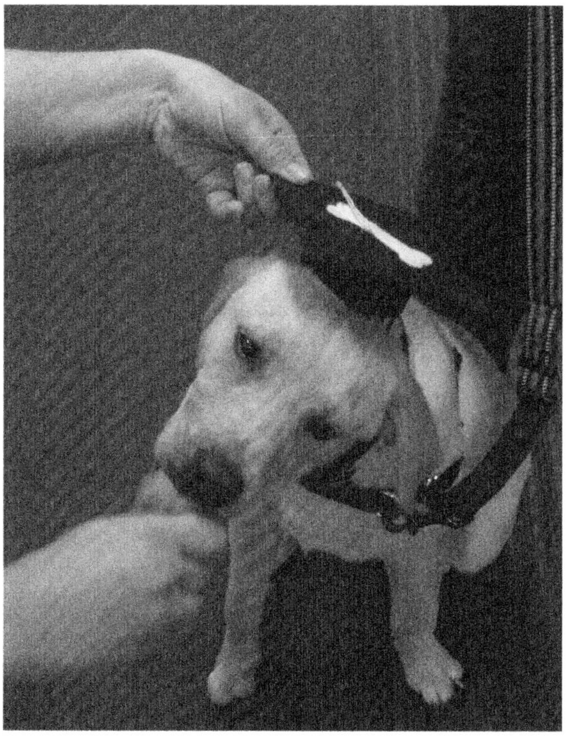

Puppy socialization: associate new/weird stuff with yummy treats.

Sensitive periods

Behavior professionals talk about "sensitive periods" (sometimes called "fear periods") in young dogs. These are times when puppies or adolescent dogs are more likely to react fearfully to new stimuli, or even to stimuli they've been exposed to in the past and were seemingly comfortable with. Although specific time periods have been identified, current thinking is that those periods are not as rigidly fixed as once thought. It is suggested that one period is around eight to twelve weeks—the time when most puppies are going to their new homes, and the time when super-socialization should be occurring. Probably a good idea to *not* ship pups by air or truck transport during this period (if ever). If your pup is coming to you from across the country, I strongly advise driving him home or arranging for another trusted person to drive him, rather than shipping him.

Later on, a dog may seem more susceptible to strong fear responses during periods that occur any time between the ages of six and 18 months. In reality, the concept of "sensitive period" is less important than responding appropriately any time your dog or puppy shows fear. Here's how to deal with fear behaviors, both during your socialization efforts and beyond:

- **Remain calm:** Dogs excel at reading our emotions and body language. If you react badly when your pup is fearful, you can compound his fear response. Stay calm and relaxed, and remember to breathe. Act as if it's no big deal, and help him out of the situation.
- **Counter-condition:** The moment your dog sees the threatening stimulus, feed high-value treats. Pause, let him look again, then feed again. Do *not* ask him to sit or watch you, just feed. You aren't giving treats for a particular behavior; you are trying to create a positive association between the scary thing and the treats. In fact, *asking* for a specific behavior can be counter-productive. You can also use counter-conditioning for scary sounds. Associate the sound with your pup's high-value treat, and he will come to love the sound. If your pup won't eat the treats, he is probably "over threshold"—the scary thing is too close, or the noise is too loud. Increase distance or find a way to turn down the volume.
- **Move away:** It is perfectly okay, in fact often advisable, to increase distance between your pup and the scary thing, until enough counter-conditioning is done to change the association from "Ooooh, scary!" to "Yay, treats!" If you find yourself having to move away frequently, it's time to up your management game so your pup doesn't keep finding himself too close to scary things.
- **Socialize:** As discussed above, socialization is your best immunization against fear. While even a well-socialized optimistic pup may go through fear periods, he will be far more resilient and recover more quickly if he has a solid foundation of socialization. While his primary socialization window may close at 13 to 14 weeks, you will want to continue to give him positive social experiences throughout his life.
- **Don't punish:** It should go without saying, but I'll say it anyway. Don't *ever* punish your dog for fear-related behaviors (or other behaviors, for that matter). He's already convinced bad things happen when that scary thing is near, and if you punish him you will confirm his suspicions and exacerbate his fear. Instead, let him know he can rely on you for support when he is scared.

So there you go. Well-socialized dogs are made, not born. Even given the genetic component, your pup's future behavioral well-being is in your hands. Take the time to super-socialize now, and your optimistic dog will confidently romp through life with you. Cut corners with your socialization program, and you and your canine pessimist are likely to pay the price in fear-related behaviors, aggression, a life full of stress, and major restrictions on what activities she can share and enjoy with you. Seems like a pretty easy choice, yes?

If you do a good job socializing your puppy, your adult dog will be happy and confident when faced with new situations.

CHAPTER 7

Upper-Level Management

Perhaps your own dog is showing some aggressive behaviors, perhaps it's a dog belonging to a friend or family member, or perhaps you're a canine behavior professional working with aggression in client dogs. Regardless of whose dog, or how serious the aggression, the first step in making sure he doesn't bite someone (or doesn't bite again) is management. Since consistency is key in any behavior modification protocol, management success requires a strong commitment by all family members.

An excellent management program is critically important to successfully working with a dog who exhibits aggressive behaviors. Note that I try not to call them "aggressive dogs." As soon as you apply a label such as "aggressive," that becomes the whole dog, and implies that it's a really bad, dangerous dog. To the contrary, *most* of my clients' canine family members are great dogs most of the time, and have gotten themselves into trouble on a few occasions. The better the client has been at *managing* the dog's environment to prevent exposure to stressors and triggers, the fewer the number of occasions.

Some trainers like to say that management always fails. I try not to say "never" or "always," as you are almost always proven wrong when you use absolutes. What I say instead is that management has a high likelihood of failing, and when choosing a management plan, you need to look at what that likelihood is, and how great the risks if management does fail. Factors that affect management failure likelihood include:

- Children in the home
- Disinterested adults in the home
- Conflict over the dog
- High-volume traffic (visitors) in and out of the home
- Ability (or lack thereof) to identify high-risk situations

- Degree of training the dog has had
- Level of persistence and determination dog has to escape or reach object of reactivity or aggression

Factors that determine the level of risk should management fail include:

- How serious prior bites have been (see Dr. Ian Dunbar's Bite Hierarchy sidebar below)
- Who the likely victim would be (child or visitor, versus adult owner choosing to assume risk)
- Outcome if dog bites again (stays in home; lawsuit; animal control involvement; rehome; euthanasia)

For example, perhaps your dog guards valuable resources. If he only guards his food bowl and/or chew toys, and the humans in the home are adult enough to know to leave him alone when he has those things, you might reasonably opt for lifetime management. Three of the four dogs in my own home will resource guard to a lesser or greater degree. We have elected simply not to bother them when they have valuable objects, and to trade in exchange for a treat should we need to get something from them.

If, however, your dog guards unpredictable random and multiple objects, and is willing to inflict significant injury in the process, then behavior modification might be in order. Or, if there are children (or adults!) in the home who aren't mature enough to understand the importance of leaving the dog alone while he eats or chews, again, modification may be necessary to keep everyone safe.

Perhaps your dog is fearful of strangers. Shut him safely away in a bedroom when visitors come over—perhaps with a padlock on the bedroom door. Still, he has to encounter strangers at least occasionally in his life—at the veterinary clinic for his annual well-pet checkup, the new pet sitter, your daughter's new boyfriend...so this one calls for at least some behavior modification, along with careful management.

As you evaluate your own dog, and your own environmental risks, make conscious educated choices about your management plans. Err on the side of caution. Always. Because dogs who bite people tend to have short lives...

Dr. Ian Dunbar's bite hierarchy

This bite hierarchy was developed by Dr. Ian Dunbar to give professionals and others a convenient and consistent means by which to identify the severity of a dog's prior bite history. Levels 1 and 2 are your dog's attempts to let you know he is uncomfortable with something, without actually inflicting damage. His communications at those levels should be taken seriously, and remedial management and modification measures put in place so he doesn't feel the need to escalate to Level 3 or higher.

- **Level 1:** Harassment but no skin contact
- **Level 2:** Tooth contact on skin but no puncture
- **Level 3:** Skin punctures; one to four holes from a single bite (all punctures shallower than length of canine)
- **Level 4:** One to four holes, deep black bruising with punctures deeper than length of canine (dog bit and clamped down), or slashes in both directions from puncture (dog bit and shook head)
- **Level 5:** Multiple bite attack with deep punctures, or multiple attack incident
- **Level 6:** Killed victim and/or consumed flesh

Management tools

There are many options for managing your dog's behavior to help him stay out of trouble. Many of them are already at your fingertips. Let's take a look.

Leash

People often don't consider a leash to be management, but think about it—you are neatly managing your dog's behavior by keeping him close to you. When you are walking your dog in public, you can combine the leash management with your verbal communications to passersby advising them to not interact with your dog. Be polite but assertive, and if necessary, drop the "polite" and just be assertive. Or even rude. Your dog's life may depend on it. In general, the "It's okay, dogs like me" people (followed closely by the "It's okay, my dog is friendly" people) are the ones most likely to get your dog into trouble—because they are so convinced dogs love them, they don't even watch for body language that may suggest otherwise.

The leash—a commonly used management tool.

Doors

If your dog doesn't love visitors, make life easier for him, for you *and* for company by closing him in a room far away from the action before your guests even arrive.

Interactive toys

Give him a KONG or other interactive toy stuffed with his dinner (soaked, if kibble) and frozen in advance, to give him something to keep him busily happy for the evening. If visitors might inadvertently open the door to your dog's safe hideaway, install a latch and padlock it.

Baby gates

Baby gates are a nice alternative to a door if your dog doesn't need the solid barrier to keep everyone safe. If, for example, your dog guards resources from his other canine siblings—or his humans—baby gates can keep everyone happily separated while they enjoy meals or their high-value chews for the day. A gate may allow your dog to be part of the social scene but still be safely separated from potential bite victims. Baby gates are not adequate management if a guest may try to reach over the gate to pet your dog and could perhaps be bitten in the process (or if your dog can jump them).

Baby gates—a handy management tool for keeping the peace.

Crates

Crates are another alternative to doors, especially if your dog crates well. It's worth taking the time to give him a good, positive introduction to his crate so you can use it as a management tool. Again, your dog can be present without being a threat to anyone. However, a dog in a crate may feel trapped and become even more defensively aggressive, so be sure the crate is located where your dog won't be harassed—either well behind a baby gate, or perhaps with an exercise pen set up as an "airlock" around him to keep people a comfortable distance away from the crate.

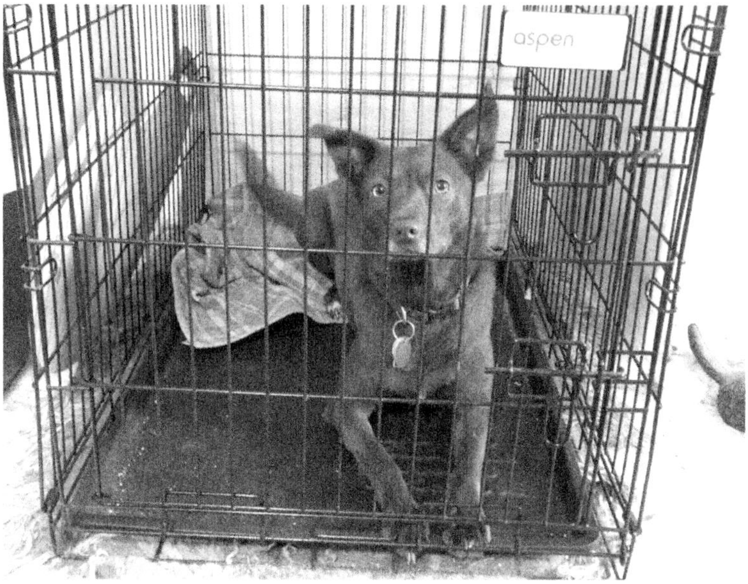

Take time to give your dog a good, positive introduction to his crate so you can use it as a management tool.

Tethers

A tether is a nice way of managing your dog without excluding him from your company. Assuming your dog accepts tethering without panicking, you can use a nylon-coated cable with snaps on both ends to tether him to a solid object—the leg of a heavy coffee table, a bed, your grand piano—or screw an eyebolt into a stud in your wall and clip him there. A third alternative is to attach a block to one end and slide it under a closed door. You can make your own tethers, or find them here: www.baddogsinc.com/product/regular-tethers. You can use a leash as a tether *if* your dog won't chew through it! Help your dog love his tether by giving him a soft bed to lie on, lots of tasty treats when you tether him, and a long-lasting chew toy to keep him occupied when tethered.

Tethering caveats: Do not tether your dog and leave him vulnerable to the unwanted attentions of humans he finds aversive—i.e., children, scary strangers, etc. Also, do not tether your dog and leave him unattended, indoors or out.

Tethering can be a valuable management tool when properly done, but dangerous if not. Note the tether around this dog's leg, which could cause injury if the dog weren't being supervised.

Boarding

If you are planning to have guests for an extended stay, consider boarding your dog for the duration, so you can relax and enjoy the visit without fretting about bite risk. Research your boarding options well—a standard boarding kennel may be too stressful for your dog (increasing the potential for a bite while kenneled), and many are not well-equipped (or trained) to properly care for dogs who have aggression issues. Your ideal choice, if you can find her, may be a positive reinforcement–based behavior professional who boards a limited number of dogs in her home. Another viable option may be a close friend or family member who knows the dog well, and with whom the dog is very comfortable, who is willing to keep the dog in her home for the duration of your guests' visit.

Medication

Medication is an important element of many successful behavior modification programs, and is also, in a way, part management. Some people are reluctant to consider medication for their canine family members, but for a dog who needs it, it is a *critically important quality of life issue.* Dogs who suffer from anxiety (which often leads to aggression) aren't having much fun, and need pharmaceutical intervention in order for their brains to even begin to understand and absorb the lessons of the modification protocol. Watch how stressed and unhappy your anxious dog is, and put yourself in his place. Then help him. Psychotropic drugs such as fluoxetine (Prozac), alprazolam (Xanax) and many others commonly used in humans, are also appropriate for behavior modification in dogs, and must be prescribed by a veterinarian. *(Note: the generic forms of these drugs are less expensive, but may not work as well as the name brand in some dogs.)* Unfortunately, most veterinarians do not study behavior in vet school, and many are not well-informed about various behavior medications (there are exceptions!). Ask your veterinarian to do a phone consultation with a veterinary behaviorist if you are considering medication for your dog, or if your non-veterinary behavior professional suggests that medication is in order. Know that medications alone will not "fix" your dog's behavior—they are intended to be used in conjunction with an appropriate behavior modification program. There are also non-prescription products—herbs, nutraceuticals and others—that purport to help decrease your dog's anxiety. Some have been studied, and studies indicate that *some* of the products *may* be useful in reducing anxiety. It's also a good idea to discuss these with your behavior professional and your veterinarian to see if they think the product(s) you are considering might be helpful, to discuss possible side effects, and to make sure they are not contraindicated due to other medications your dog might be taking. Some commonly used non-prescription calming products include:

- **L-theanine:** A nutraceutical found in green tea, an amino acid found primarily in particular plant and fungal species
- **C3—Colostrum Calming Complex:** A branded blend of ten different peptides derived from colostrum
- **Lactium:** A milk protein hydrolysate containing a bioactive peptide with anti-stress properties
- **Zylkene:** Derived from casein, a protein in milk that has calming properties
- **Herbs:** Valerian root, passion flower, skullcap, chamomile

Muzzles

Muzzles deserve a more in-depth discussion than some of the other management tools, because they are easily misused. While a muzzle can be a valuable tool for keeping people and other dogs safe from your dog's potential bite, let's be clear about one thing right from the start. A muzzle won't train your dog. It will not teach your dog not to bite, nor will it teach him to love small children, tall men with beards, hats and umbrellas, or your veterinarian. A muzzle is a behavior management tool, properly used as a temporary measure to protect humans (or other dogs) when dogs *have to be* handled in situations that are too stressful for them to tolerate. A muzzle is also a flashing neon warning sign that it's time to do some serious behavior modification so the dog in question can be handled in normal situations without resorting to muzzling. Dogs should *not* have to muzzled for basic vet exams, grooming, nail trimming or other routine maintenance procedures.

A muzzle is also definitely *not* a license to immerse your dog in situations where, if he weren't muzzled, someone would be bitten. Do *not* muzzle your dog who bites children and turn him loose in the middle of your son's birthday party. Do *not* muzzle your dog-aggressive dog and take him to the dog park. Do *not* muzzle your fear-aggressive dog and invite strangers to pet him. Doing any of these things will *sensitize* him *more* to his triggers, and ultimately make him *more* likely to bite, not less.

However, there are times when muzzles are useful. They can provide safety zones for us to implement desensitization and training programs for aggressive dogs without risking our own lives and limbs. (Note: a dog who will be wearing a muzzle as part of a training program needs to be acclimated to the muzzle so that he thinks the muzzle is wonderful. Otherwise you are adding a significant stressor and moving him closer to his bite threshold, making bites *more* likely rather than *less* likely.) Muzzles can keep our animal care professionals safe when an aggressive dog *must* (regrettably) be treated for an illness or injury prior to the successful completion of a behavior modification program. (Bear in mind that this is likely to cause a setback in the training program.) And even a well-socialized, friendly dog may bite when injured, so a muzzle is always appropriate when handling a dog who may be in pain.

There are two basic types of muzzles—sleeve muzzles and basket muzzles. Many veterinarians seem to prefer sleeve muzzles, but a basket muzzle is the preferred choice for behavior modification. Basket muzzles are more comfortable for the dog—he can breathe normally, and you can feed treats through the basket. If you bring your dog to your veterinary clinic calmly wearing his basket muzzle, chances are good your veterinarian will be happily comfortable with your choice. You might even discuss it with her in advance to be sure she will accommodate your muzzle wishes.

The important qualities of a muzzle are:

- Comfort for the dog
- Safety for the dog
- Ability for the dog to breathe normally, take treats and drink water
- Ease and safety of application and adjustment
- Security once in place on the dog
- Effectiveness in preventing biting
- Durability for long-term use
- Cost

Your goal is to condition your dog to love his muzzle. If he already has one he dislikes, get a new muzzle—different brand, different style—and start conditioning.

Conditioning your dog to love his muzzle

1. Begin by holding the muzzle up a few feet from your dog in one hand. With the other hand, deliver a bit of very high-value treat, such as chicken—baked, boiled or canned. Then put muzzle and chicken behind your back.

2. Repeat Step 1 many times. Each time, present the muzzle first, *then* bring out your chicken hand and feed a tidbit of chicken, then hide both behind your back again. You are working to convince your dog's brain that the muzzle makes chicken appear, so the muzzle has to come first.

3. Eventually you will notice that, when you bring out the muzzle, your dog's head swivels to look for the chicken hand. This is called a **conditioned emotional response** (CER) and it tells you that he has made the association: muzzle makes chicken happen. When he does this consistently, begin offering the muzzle a few inches closer.

4. Repeat, gradually moving the muzzle closer, and obtaining a consistent CER at each new distance, until the muzzle is next to his face.

5. Now begin feeding treats through the end of the muzzle so he pokes his nose into the basket to get the treat. Repeat until he is offering to place his nose into the muzzle when you hold it up, even before you put treats at the end.

6. Continue this process with the remainder of the mechanics of putting the muzzle on. *Tip: you can smear peanut butter or squeeze cheese on your refrigerator door to keep him happily occupied while you fumble with straps and get the muzzle buckled.* If at any point in the process he backs away, seems reluctant or fearful, you have moved too quickly. Back up several steps in the process and continue again, moving forward more slowly this time. If you prefer not to smear stuff on your refrigerator, try the Chase and Chomp Sticky Bone: *http://www.caitec.com/product-p/711085600527.htm*

7. When you can hold up the muzzle and your dog happily runs to you to put it on, and happily wears it when you walk him on leash, you've done your job.

8. As you use the muzzle from time to time for scary vet visits, etc., be sure to continue doing "happy muzzle" sessions at home with high-value treats so the muzzle doesn't always predict an aversive event.

CHAPTER 8

Modifying Aggressive Behavior

Whether you are a dedicated and capable dog owner working with your dog's aggressive behavior on your own, or a professional working to modify the aggressive behavior of clients' dogs, it's useful to have a procedure that you follow to make sure you are thorough and not missing any of the important elements of a successful behavior modification program. Here is the framework that I follow for my aggression cases. Note that the actual work of behavior modification is just a small part of this plan. Thorough assessment of the behavior and a management strategy for keeping everyone safe while behavior modification is undertaken are key components as well.

Building a behavior modification plan

1. **Description of behavior:** Create (for your own dog) or obtain (for a client's dog) a complete description of the problem behavior(s). You want descriptions, not conclusions. Example: "My dog barks and lunges at the window, sometimes actually crashing into the window, when people pass by the house on the sidewalk" (a description of what the dog does and when he does it), not "My dog is very territorial and so he barks whenever anyone comes near the house" (a conclusion about why the dog is acting this way or what he is thinking). It is best to use very neutral language that describes actual behaviors (barking, lunging, growling, etc.). Even a description like "My dog goes crazy when people pass by the house on the sidewalk" could be interpreted many different ways. Stick to the facts, and be as specific as possible.

2. **Management:** Immediately put management measures securely in place to prevent recurrence of the aggressive behavior. If something you are doing is triggering the aggression, stop doing it. If something or someone else is triggering the aggression, prevent your dog's access to that

person or thing, and prevent that person or thing from having access to your dog. Example: Block your dog's access to the windows, or cover the windows with an opaque film so he can't see passersby.

3. **Medical:** Do a full medical workup to rule out or identify and treat any medical conditions. Medical issues can be huge contributors to aggressive behavior. If your vet is not behaviorally knowledgeable (and many are not), insist that s/he contact a veterinary behaviorist to identify what should be included in a "full medical workup" for behavior purposes.

4. **Identify the type of behavior:** Determine the nature of the aggression you are working with (remember that fear-related aggression is most common). This will help you determine how best to proceed with your behavior modification program.

5. **Educate yourself:** Access reliable sources to educate yourself (or a client) about the behavior. If you are uncertain about the reliability of the source, ask a qualified force-free behavior professional. Education may include learning about breed propensities (i.e., the herding breeds have a strong genetic propensity to chase and try to control things that move, such as children), and dispelling myths about behavior (no, your dog isn't being "alpha" and you don't have to dominate him).

6. **Identify realistic goals:** Behavior is almost always modifiable, at least to some degree, but you may not be able to completely eliminate your dog's behavioral challenges. For example, your dog-aggressive/reactive dog will probably never be a candidate for dog-park play, but it is likely that you can help him become appropriate in normal social encounters, such as passing another dog on the sidewalk on leash. Your Border Collie will probably always want to herd and nip at things that move quickly, but with some solid good manners training and appropriate management you should be able to control her herding impulses around your child and your child's friends.

7. **List stressors, assign strategies, determine priorities:** As described earlier, identify the dog's stressors, assign appropriate strategies to each stressor, and determine which are your priorities. Priorities should include getting rid of any stressors that are disposable (throw away the shock collar, penny can and verbal/physical punishments; treat medical conditions; don't let brother-in-law tease the dog, etc.), as well as the clear and obvious triggers for the aggression. Aside from the "get rid of" and "manage" stressors, it is reasonable to actively work on modification for two to four stressors concurrently (but in different work sessions).

8. **Select/create a modification plan for priority stressors:** If you select counter-conditioning for one or more stressors, determine threshold intensity of stimulus for that stressor, and decide how, when and where you will do the work. I recommend a minimum of 20 minutes per session for counter-conditioning unless things are going very badly, in which case, abort the session and try again another day with a greatly decreased intensity of stimulus. I ask my clients for a time commitment for each stressor we select. They tell me what is reasonable for them. It might be that three 20-minute sessions per day would accomplish the most successful behavior modification, but if I tell them they have to do that and they can't, chances are they'll give up and not do anything at all. I'd rather that they tell me what they can do and we work from there. A "commitment" might look like this for a client with a dog who is fearful of/aggressive toward children: A minimum of three times per week, 20 minutes per session, do counter-conditioning with children at a safe/sub-threshold distance. (More is fine/better.) We agreed you would do this for now with children at the safely fenced daycare center up the block from your home. The fence will keep the children contained and you can work at whatever distance is appropriate to keep your dog comfortably below threshold, gradually moving closer as long as your dog is doing well.

9. **Implement the plan:** *Professionals*—Before ending your initial session with a client, be sure to practice each of the procedures the client is agreeing to work on. Demonstrate if you can (if the dog will work with you) and then be sure to have the client practice so you can coach her on the mechanics of the procedures. *Dog owners*—Be sure you have a solid understanding of what you plan to do with your dog. Practice the mechanics of the procedure(s) in a safe environment *before* you venture out for your first real-world attempt, so you are comfortable with how to hold the leash and feed chicken at the same time.

10. **Write a report/keep a behavior log:** *Professionals*—Take thorough notes during your session with your client, and upon returning to your office, write a detailed report that summarizes the topics you discussed and the action plan agreed upon by you and the client. A copy of this should be provided to your client within a day or two of your session. *Dog owners*—Take notes after each session with your dog, detailing times, places, distances and results. This will help you evaluate your progress and determine if changes are needed to the program. It will also help you look back at some point in the future and realize how much progress you have made.

11. **Evaluate/modify program as needed:** *Professionals*—Ask your clients to check in with you at a designated time period (I usually ask for a report from the client in two weeks), while reassuring them they can contact you at any time—they don't have to wait the two weeks. Advise them to stop immediately and let you know if anything they've agreed to do seems to be making the behavior worse instead of better. Based on their feedback, determine if they should proceed with the program, or if alterations are needed. *Dog owners*—Keep a behavior journal so you can track your dog's progress. Whether working with a professional or working on your own, if you're seeing good progress, carry on. If behavior isn't improving, consider how to modify the program for better success.

Behavior analysis

The process of "behavior analysis" is well-known in the field of behavior. It involves understanding what triggers and motivates a behavior in order to change behavior using management and manipulation of reinforcers, and is sometimes called the "ABC Formula":

A = Antecedent: Whatever occurs prior to the behavior that causes the behavior to happen.

B = Behavior: The behavior in question that is being addressed.

C = Consequence: How behavior is impacted—either a good thing happens (is reinforcing and tends to increase) or a bad thing happens (is punishing and tends to decrease).

By preventing the antecedent from occurring (management) or changing the consequence, we can change behavior.

Behavioral modification techniques

These are the modification techniques that I recommend depending on the particular behaviors of your dog:

- Counter-conditioning
- Operant conditioning
    - Constructional Aggression Treatment
    - Behavior Adjustment Training

Counter-conditioning

Counter-conditioning involves changing your dog's association with a scary or arousing stimulus (the thing that causes a behavioral response) from negative to positive. This is the protocol I use most commonly to modify a dog's aggressive behavior because it is simple and effective when properly done. The easiest way to give most dogs a positive association is with *very high-value, really yummy treats.* I like to use chicken—canned, baked or boiled, since most dogs love chicken and it's a low-fat, low-calorie food, so it's generally healthy for them as well.

Here's how the process works with a dog:

1. Determine the distance at which your dog can be in the presence of the stimulus and be alert or wary but not extremely fearful or aroused. This is called the threshold distance. It could be ten feet, or it could be 100 feet. Or more.

2. With you holding your dog on leash, have a helper present the stimulus at threshold distance X. The instant your dog sees the stimulus, start feeding bits of chicken. Feed, then pause so she can look at the stimulus again, and as soon as she does, feed chicken again. Repeat several times.

3. After several seconds, have the helper remove the stimulus, and stop feeding chicken.

4. Keep repeating Steps 1 through 3 until the presentation of the stimulus at that distance consistently causes your dog to look at you with a happy smile and a "Yay! Where's my chicken?" expression. This is a conditioned emotional response (CER)—the physical manifestation of your dog's new association with the stimulus. Your dog's association with the stimulus at threshold distance X is now positive instead of negative.

Now you need to increase the intensity of the stimulus. I'd suggest you begin by decreasing distance in small increments by moving the dog diagonally closer to the location where the stimulus will appear as in Steps 5 and 6 below, achieving your CER at each new distance. Then increase until the amount of time spent at each distance as in Step 7. When done this way, your dog will gradually become happy to be very near to the non-moving stimulus, perhaps even sniffing or targeting to it (see Targeting in Chapter 10).

You can do that by:

- Decreasing distance to X minus Y
- Increasing movement of the stimulus at distance X (a child walking, skipping or swinging her arms instead of standing still)
- Increasing the number of stimuli (two or three children, instead of one);
- Increasing the visual "threat" (a tall man instead of a short one, or a man with a beard instead of a clean-shaven one)
- Increasing duration (the length of time the stimulus is visible), or by increasing volume (if it's a stimulus that makes noise, such as a vacuum cleaner)

5. Then return to distance X and increase the intensity of your stimulus again (move the vacuum a little, have two children instead of one, have the man put on a hat or a backpack), gradually decreasing distance and attaining CERs along the way, until your dog is delighted to have the moderately intense stimulus in close proximity.

6. Now, back to distance X, increase intensity again, by having your helper turn the vacuum on briefly, feed treats the instant it's on, then turn it off and stop the treats. (Or turn up the volume, or add more children, etc.)

7. Repeat until you have the CER, then gradually increase the length of time you have your dog in the presence of the increased-intensity stimulus until he's happy (but not aroused) to have it present continuously.

8. Begin decreasing distance in small increments, moving the dog closer to the stimulus, obtaining your CER consistently at each new distance.

9. When your dog is happy to have the higher-intensity stimulus close to him, you're ready for the final phase. Return to distance X and obtain your CER there, with a full intensity stimulus—a running, moving vacuum; multiple children laughing and playing; a tall man with a beard wearing a hat, sunglasses and a backpack. Then gradually decrease distance until your dog is happy to be in the presence of your full-intensity stimulus. He now thinks the stimulus is a very good thing, as a reliable predictor of very yummy treats. In the case of a human stimulus, you can gradually work up to actual interaction with the human(s) at this stage, by having the person(s) drop treats as they walk by, then letting the dog take treats from their fingers—without direct eye contact, and eventually working up to normal interaction.

Feed high-value treats to give your dog a positive association with an aversive stimulus.

You can use counter-conditioning to give your dog a happy association (ponies make chicken happen!) with other animals.

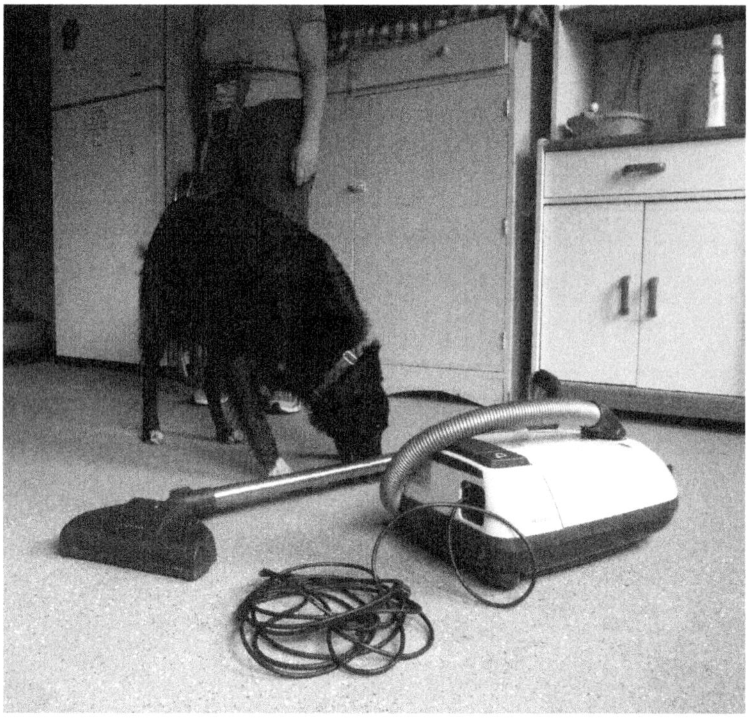

Counter-conditioning can work to give your dog a new, happy association with scary household appliances such as vacuum cleaners (vacuum cleaners make chicken happen!).

The more complex the stimulus and the more intense the fear or arousal response, the more challenging the behavior is to modify. Anxieties and phobias generally require a greater commitment to a longer-term and more in-depth modification program.

In order to stress the importance of *high-value treats,* staying below threshold, and gradual increase in intensity of stimulus, I often use this analogy with my clients: Let's say you are phobic of snakes. I set you in a chair at one end of an 80-foot-long room, and at the opposite end of the room I hold up a photograph of a snake. A $100 bill drops into your lap. Woo hoo! I keep repeating this step until every time I hold up the photo you look up at the ceiling in anticipation of the $100 bill that's about to fall. This is your CER.

Now I gradually move closer, continuing to pair the presentation of the photo with money falling from the sky. Then I start back again at the 80-foot distance, this time with a realistic rubber snake, and repeat the whole process. Then I use a tiny, harmless garter snake in a padlocked, shatter-proof tank and do it all again. Then I bring the tiny snake out of the tank, and repeat the process, adding in a step of having you actually touch, then hold the snake. I gradually increase the size of the snake until you are happily sitting in your chair with an eight-foot boa constrictor coiled in your arms. You have been counter-conditioned (and you are now a very wealthy person!).

Using food in counter-conditioning

Your job is to find your dog's food equivalent of a $100 bill. (Hint—this would not have worked if a penny fell from the ceiling into your lap each time I held up the snake instead of a $100 bill.) Food is commonly used to counter-condition, because it's hard to eat yummy treats and be significantly angry or afraid at the same time. Food is a **primary reinforcer**—we (and our dogs) are genetically pre-programmed to like food; we don't have to *learn* that it's valuable to us and our survival. Think chocolate—or whatever your own favorite comfort food is. But you can use other things to change associations in place of, or in addition to, food. With humans, money, jewelry and other **conditioned reinforcers** (items with *learned* value) can be used to create and change associations. Think of the enamored suitor, wooing the object of his affections, plying her with all sorts of goodies to create a positive association while she plays hard-to-get. Dogs aren't much impressed with diamonds and Cadillacs, but a rousing game of tug or fetch-the-ball can give a worried dog a positive association with a previously aversive stimulus.

Trouble-shooting your counter-conditioning efforts

There are some common errors I often see when someone is trying to do counter-conditioning:

- **Value of treats too low:** Remember, use $100 bills, not pennies.
- **Aversive stimulus too close:** A very common error is having the scary/aggression-inducing person feed high-value treats to the dog. This puts the aversive stimulus (child, man with beard, etc.) far too close to the dog. The dog may want the treat very badly, so he approaches, focused on the treat, not the person. But as soon as he eats the treat he realizes that the person is too close, and BAM, the bite happens. Good intentions, but faulty application.

Make sure you start your counter-conditioning program with the aversive stimulus far enough away that your dog will stay below threshold—he should take treats easily, and not bark and lunge.

- **Improper sequencing:** For the most effective counter-conditioning, the high-value treat must *immediately follow* the presentation of the aversive stimulus. You want the dog to realize the scary thing makes the treats appear. If you feed treats first you may succeed in keeping the dog distracted and below threshold, but you're not doing as good a job of creating the new association.
- **Rewarding/asking for behavior:** With **operant conditioning,** the dog's behavior makes the treat happen. (I sit, I get a cookie.) We use operant conditioning a lot in training. Some people mistakenly muddle this with the counter-conditioning protocol used for behavior modification, where the presence of the aversive stimulus makes treats happen, not the dog's behavior. Of course, you want to keep your dog below threshold so you aren't inadvertently reinforcing unwanted behavior. If your dog is barking, lunging or simply too tense to take treats, the intensity of the stimulus is too high. You are too close, there are too many of the scary things, there is too much movement, the volume is too high. Move farther away, reduce the number of children or have them stand still, turn down the volume, or find some other way to decrease the intensity of the stimulus. Some people also beseech their dog to "Watch me!" when the aversive stimulus is passing, and reinforce the dog for eye contact. With counter-conditioning you *want* your dog to look at the scary thing, and feed as soon as he looks, then let him look again, feed again, over and over. Think about it. Let's say you are terrified of dragons. Will you feel better if you can repeatedly look at the dragon to see where he is, or if you have to keep your back to the dragon and wonder if he is getting closer?
- **Increasing intensity of stimulus too quickly:** We are an impatient species, and we like to see results. When counter-conditioning is done properly, the dog stays calm and below threshold—you don't see anything other than the dog's repeated looks to you for chicken. Some people feel like nothing is happening, and they decrease distance (or otherwise increase intensity of stimulus) too quickly. The dog goes over threshold, and there's a setback in the program. Take your time. Err on the side of caution. You will make progress faster if you go slowly. Start each new session at a significantly lower intensity of stimulus than you ended the last one. If you think you're going too slowly...slow down.

Operant conditioning

You *can* use operant conditioning to modify aggressive behavior as well. With operant conditioning, the dog makes a deliberate behavior choice in order to affect the outcome. "I sit, I get a cookie—therefore I will choose to sit more." "I bark and lunge at the delivery person, the delivery person goes away—therefore I will bark and lunge more at the delivery person." Two operant methods for modifying aggression are the CAT (Constructional Aggression Treatment) and BAT (Behavior Adjustment Training) protocols. Although aggression is initially a classically conditioned emotional response (dog has made a negative association with children, men with beards, skateboarders, etc.), there is also an operant component.

Dogs want to make good stuff happen, and they want to make bad stuff go away. A lot like us! When the *emotional* part of a fearful dog's brain (the amygdala) reacts in response to his emotions by triggering a bark and lunge at a scary person, the person usually goes away. The *thinking* part of the dog's brain (the cortex) says, "Note to self: I can make scary people go away by barking and lunging at them." Over time, the aggressive response to that stimulus becomes more deliberate and less *just* an emotional response. The dog has learned a strategy that, in his mind, works to keep him safe.

The four principles of operant conditioning

Operant conditioning is a basic element of the science of behavior and learning. It says that all living things repeat behaviors that are rewarding to them, and avoid behaviors that make bad things happen. Note that, in these terms, "positive" and "negative" refer to things being *added to* or *taken away from* the dog's environment (rather than meaning "pleasant" and "unpleasant"). Reinforcement makes a behavior increase, and punishment makes it decrease. Thus, the four principles of operant conditioning are:

Positive Reinforcement (+R): The dog's behavior makes a good thing happen, so the behavior increases: he sits, and you give him a treat. He likes getting treats, so he sits more.

Positive Punishment (+P): The dog's behavior makes a bad thing happen, so the behavior decreases: he jumps up and you knee him in the chest *(this procedure is not recommended!).* He doesn't like a knee in the chest, so he jumps up less.

Negative Punishment (-P): The dog's behavior makes a good thing go away, so the behavior decreases: when he jumps up to grab the ball from your hand, you hide the ball behind your back. He doesn't want the ball to go away, so he jumps up less. (When he sits, you throw the ball [+R] so he sits more and jumps up less. Negative punishment works best if you follow it with positive reinforcement for the behavior you want instead.)

Negative Reinforcement (-R): The dog's behavior makes a bad thing go away. Your puppy struggles when restrained, so you hold him until he becomes calm, and then let him go. He doesn't want to be restrained, so he learns to be calm in order to make restraint go away *(this procedure is not recommended!).*

Carefully applied in the CAT and BAT procedures, you can use operant conditioning to teach your dog that calm, relaxed behaviors make scary things go away. When the dog deliberately becomes calm and relaxed he is no longer fearful, and no longer has the need to make those things go away.

Constructional Aggression Treatment (CAT)

Dr. Jesus Rosales-Ruiz is a behavior analyst and associate professor of behavior analysis at the University of North Texas. Kellie Snider is a board-certified associate behavior analyst and protégé of Dr. Rosales-Ruiz. She completed her MS in behavior analysis at UNT in early 2008. Together, the pair devised and tested a shaping-based operant protocol that, they suggest, produces stronger and much faster results than the classical counter-conditioning process widely used by training and behavior professionals.

How does CAT work?

The subject dog—the one with the aggressive behavior, is set up in an area where the trigger stimulus, let's say another dog, can be presented at a distance—preferably sub-threshold. Ideally, the environment is the same one in which the undesirable behavior normally occurs, or at least very similar. This reduces the amount of future **generalization** (helping the dog understand that the behavior, training or modification process works everywhere, not just in the original training environment) required. The owner holds the dog's leash, not a trainer—again, keeping the stimulus picture as close to reality as possible, and reducing the amount of generalization needed. Other than restraining the dog, the owner does nothing else in terms of training—no clicking, no treating. The behavior of the stimulus dog becomes the sole reinforcer for the subject dog's behavior.

The neutral dog, with handler, approaches the subject dog until sub-threshold signs of stress are noted by observers. This is the **baseline distance.** The handler and neutral dog stop, and wait for *any* decrease in the subject dog's stress behavior, at which point the neutral dog and handler immediately turn and walk away, reinforcing the subject dog's more appropriate (less stressed) behavior with the increase in distance. If the subject dog barks, lunges or offers other aggressive behavior as the neutral dog leaves, the handler and neutral dog immediately return to baseline to again wait for decreased signs of stress. Then they again attempt to leave. This is repeated until the subject dog no longer offers escalated stress behavior when the neutral dog and handler attempt to leave. When this happens, they retreat to a greater distance to give the subject dog an opportunity to relax, and move the baseline mark farther away from the subject dog.

An assistant marks the baseline spot, and the neutral dog and handler return to the baseline mark after a 15-second "cool-down" period. This return-and-leave process continues until the subject dog no longer shows any signs of stress at baseline, at which point the handler brings the neutral dog closer to the subject by a distance predetermined by the trainer—less if the dog is likely to be easily triggered, more if the dog is perceived as able to handle a larger increment of decreased distance. Eventually the neutral dog is able to approach with no aggressive reaction from the subject. In fact, in a successful procedure the subject dog begins to genuinely and happily *invite* the neutral dog closer for more interaction, offering distance-decreasing behaviors such as tail wags, squinty eyes and play bows. This point in the procedure is called **switchover**.

After switchover, neutral dog and handler continue to approach the subject dog in increments until the two dogs can actually engage in friendly behavior with each other. The researchers labeled this part of the process **interaction**.

Why does CAT work?

The subject dog offers aggressive behaviors because he has learned that acting aggressively makes the trigger stimulus—in this case another dog—go away. Because that behavior has proven to be successful in the past, it's been reinforced, and the behavior has continued or increased. With CAT, the subject dog is being presented with a different reinforcement scenario. The behavior that worked so well before—barking and lunging—is no longer working. Instead of making the other dog go away, it actually makes her come back! A new behavior—acting calm—now makes the "bad approaching dog" go away. So, in theory, the subject dog learns to offer calm, relaxed behaviors to make the other dog go away. Eventually the subject dog *becomes* calm and relaxed because he no longer needs to act aggressive to make the other dog go away. Lo and behold, once the subject dog *becomes* calm and relaxed about the other dog approaching, he actually gets *happy* about having other dogs approach—his emotional response change follows his behavioral response change.

Rosales-Ruiz and Snider have worked with or received reports of hundreds of dogs using the CAT procedure, and the results, they say, are overwhelmingly encouraging. Dogs with a lifetime history of aggression toward other dogs have become completely canine-social-appropriate. Dogs with a long record of aggression toward humans have become safe and friendly. Not every single one, of course, but the vast majority of reported CAT dogs have done mind-bogglingly well with the procedure.

As striking as the reported results may seem, there are some significant potential obstacles to the widespread use of CAT. Trainers who might consider using this procedure professionally are struggling with some of the challenges:

1. It's intensively time consuming. Individual CAT sessions may run from as short as one hour to as long as eight. Snider suggests setting aside three full days to work with an individual dog and owner.

2. It's costly. Good training and behavior professionals may charge anywhere from 50 to hundreds of dollars per hour for their time. Three full days, eight hours per day, at hundreds of dollars per hour equals *a lot of money.*

3. It's staff intensive. Done well, the procedure requires at least several humans—the owner, the trainer, the handlers of several neutral dogs (or presenters of whatever the trigger stimulus may be), and perhaps a person to videotape the procedure for later review. This can also add to the cost, if assistants are paid.

4. It can be stressful to the subject dog. In some cases where the procedure has failed, the subject dog has continued to practice the bark/lunge strategy that's been successful for him in the past, rather than offering—and switching over to—calm, relaxed behavior. Some trainers trying the procedure have pulled the plug early in the process rather than continue

to subject the dog to the level of stress apparent as the old strategy failed to work. Other trainers have persisted for inordinately long periods of time (hours) before either giving up or ultimately achieving success.

5. It can be stressful to the neutral dog. If the subject dog continues to react, the neutral dog is repeatedly being asked to approach a dog who is sending very clear "DON'T APPROACH" signals, and appears to be more than willing to back the signals up. This can take a toll on the good nature of the neutral dog.

6. Even when all goes according to plan, trainers may be reluctant to complete the final piece of the process—interaction—and rightly so. The ethical concern that a misjudgment on the part of the trainer could result in injury to the neutral dog (or trigger person(s)) is not one to be dismissed lightly.

7. Some feel it may not be positive. One definition of "positive training" holds the position that positive trainers use negative reinforcement only as a last resort, after positive reinforcement and negative punishment have failed. Negative reinforcement, by definition, requires the presentation of something at least mildly aversive to the dog (so does counter-conditioning!), and sometimes the presenting stimulus is significantly aversive. Snider and Rosales-Ruiz offer CAT as a first approach, not after exhausting what are traditionally considered more positive methods. In fact, they say the less the dog has been worked with using other methods, the easier and more successful CAT is likely to be.

After implementing the CAT procedure with several client dogs I can say this: It works well with a lot of dogs. Like any training or behavior modification approach, it doesn't work with *every* dog. It also requires a commitment on the part of the dog's human to take the procedure and generalize it—a challenge that can require some creative thinking and planning on the owner's part.

For more about the CAT procedure, go to: *www.youtube.com/watch?v=XdnED053tDw* or see these two DVDs: *Constructional Aggression Treatment—C.A.T. for Dogs* (Tawzer, with Kellie Snider and Dr. Jesus Rosales Ruiz) or my own DVD—*Juni's C.A.T. Procedure.*

Charlie the Beagle, reactive toward other dogs, does the CAT procedure with Scooter the Pomeranian, and learns that being calm and relaxed makes Scooter go away.

Calm and relaxed, Charlie no longer feels the need to make Scooter go away, and can interact appropriately with him. Scooter is a little concerned about Charlie's approach (behind the vertical/backing away) but soon recovers and is able to walk happily next to him.

They can even walk together, with Charlie unconcerned about Scooter's proximity.

Behavior Adjustment Training (BAT)

The BAT procedure was developed by trainer Grisha Stewart, author of *Behavior Adjustment Training,* as an alternative to the CAT procedure, which she felt had the potential to be too aversive to dogs. With the BAT procedure, the aversive (scary) stimulus is stationary, and the subject dog is allowed to approach the stimulus. In the original version of BAT, the handler watches for a **cut-off signal**—body language that tells the handler the dog would prefer to increase distance from the scary thing, such as sniffing the ground or looking back at the handler. The handler can prompt the dog to increase distance when necessary to keep the dog below threshold (if the dog doesn't offer a signal). According to Stewart in her book, "BAT empowers animals to live with confidence and joy among humans." She also states that "By setting up situations in which dogs can safely explore the environment and investigate other dogs, people, etc., BAT helps dogs learn to control their own comfort level through peaceful means."

BAT has evolved substantially since its inception in 2009. It now gives the dog even more freedom of choice in his movements, and can best be understood in its current format via Stewart's most recent book, *Behavior Adjustment Training 2.0.*

When training, I use a variation of BAT that I prefer; I like to install a specific cut-off signal first by doing counter-conditioning with the aversive stimulus, as demonstrated to me by trainer Sean Howard, PMCT, CPDT-KA, of Up With Pup in Toronto, Canada. The CER "Where's my chicken?" look becomes the cut-off signal. This is different than the BAT methodology promoted by Stewart, but I find this works well. With a dog-reactive dog, it might look like this:

1. With the neutral dog(s) far enough away that the subject dog stays below threshold (is not excessively stressed, barking, lunging, etc.) do the counter-conditioning sequence (look-feed, look-feed) until the dog is

regularly offering CERs. We will call this baseline. The neutral dogs could be dogs playing in a fenced dog park, as long as they are not free to approach the subject dog.

2. Set up cones (or some other markers), with the first cone at baseline, the remainder in a line pointing toward the neutral dog(s), spaced at a distance appropriate for the dog you are working with. (Some dogs can decrease distance in large increments [one to two feet], others need to decrease distance by mere inches.) The markers will help you prevent your dog from venturing too close.
3. Invite your dog to move to the first cone. You want him to move forward willingly. If he chooses not to move forward, you are too close. Move your baseline farther away from the other dogs.
4. When he gets to the first cone, stop and wait for him to look toward you—even slightly. Mark the look with a "Yes!" run 15 to 20 feet away, feed him several treats and have a happy party.
5. Repeat multiple times, approaching the first cone, waiting for the look, then running away for a happy party.
6. When there is clearly no sign of tension at the first cone, invite the dog to proceed to the second cone and repeat the steps, then the third cone, and so on.

BAT works because the dog realizes he can choose to move away from the aversive stimulus (in this case, other dogs) whenever he wants, and so becomes less stressed about their presence. When the BAT procedure is successful, the dog eventually becomes calm and relaxed in the normal social presence of the previously aversive stimulus.

I have used this version of BAT successfully with several dogs, and find it a useful choice for some situations—such as when a modification program seems to have plateaued with counter-conditioning. One of the advantages of the BAT program is that it requires a less formal set-up than the CAT procedure, and can be easier for a dog owner to implement without excessive assistance by a behavior professional.

Trainer Beth Brock's Border Collie, Domino, was initially quite concerned about this pig statue hidden in the shadow. You can see that Domino's ears are pricked forward, indicating his significant level of concern.

On the next attempted approach, note that Domino is more relaxed and glances up at Beth rather than staring at the pig which signals to Beth that he would like to move away now.

Beth marks Domino's behavior for requesting to leave by saying "Good Boy."

Then parties and feeds treats.

And runs away with him for another party at the starting point.

SECTION III

Aggression: Classifications, Discussions and Practical Applications

In this section I will present a classification of the various types of aggression followed in detail by several different examples of common aggression presentations to give you a more in-depth understanding of how to create a protocol for your dog's specific behavior. While I won't address every possible presentation of aggression, I will provide enough information that you should be able to tailor the protocols to your own dog's behavior. If you find that you do need the assistance of a qualified behavior professional, I have provided guidelines for doing that in Chapter 18 and in the Appendix. Chapter 19 covers the subject of rehoming, and Chapter 20 discusses the importance of advocating for your dog, and how best to do that.

CHAPTER 9

Classification of Aggression

We used to put a lot of emphasis on classifications of aggression, yet to this day the behavior field doesn't have a universal, agreed-upon list of classifications. You can find various lists and definitions in a variety of sources, and it *can* be useful at times to have a label for the presentation of aggression (so people can call it something *other* than "dominance"), but what's more important than a name is an effective protocol for managing and modifying the aggression, whatever the cause.

Bearing in mind that classifications of aggression are not universally agreed upon in the behavior field, and that proper treatment is more important than a label, here is one example of common classifications for aggressive behavior:

- **Fear aggression (Chapter 10)**
    - Dog may cower and try to escape; dangerous if cornered
    - May bite from behind and run away
    - Can be induced by punishment or association with pain
    - May shake and tremble
    - May bark and growl while backing away
- **Idiopathic aggression (Chapter 17)**
    - No identifiable context
    - Very rare
    - Usually misdiagnosed impulse-control aggression
- **Impulse-control aggression (Chapter 16)**
    - Occurs during human attempts to actively or passively control dog's behavior

  - Usually appears at social maturity (12 to 36 months of age)
  - Has also been called "dominance aggression," "conflict aggression" and "social aggression" (The term "dominance aggression" is no longer considered correct by many behavior professionals, including the author.)
- **Inter-dog aggression (Chapter 15)**
  - Most commonly same-sex (male-male or female-female) but not always
  - Usually appears at social maturity (12 to 36 months of age)
  - May start as stares, bumps, mounting or body blocks
  - Older or weaker dog may be victimized
- **Maternal aggression**
  - Protects pups, toys, bedding from people or other dogs
  - If constantly threatened, may eat pup or toy
- **Pain-related aggression**
  - Can be response to actual pain or anticipated pain, related to touch or manipulation
  - May grab hands in attempt to stop pain or anticipated pain
  - May be in response to rough play from humans (especially children) or other dogs, particularly if dog is old/arthritic
  - Can progress to fear aggression
- **Play aggression**
  - Different from aggressive play, but can occur when rough play escalates beyond playmate dog's tolerance level; dog uncomfortable with play becomes aggressive to try to stop escalation when other dog doesn't heed signals
  - Can also result from increased arousal in play with humans—rough play escalates to dog's mouth on human skin and clothing.
- **Possession aggression/food-related aggression (Chapters 13 and 14)**
  - Also called "resource guarding"
  - Will not relinquish valuable objects or food—may be his, or objects/food he is not supposed to have
  - Growling on approach of human or other dog—can be extremely long distance
  - Can be fiercely dangerous
  - Part/early indicator of control complex involving impulse-control aggression

- **Predatory aggression (Chapter 12)**
    - Not true aggression, is food-obtaining behavior—although result to victim can be very serious/fatal
    - May track and stalk or chase victims: small animals, children, joggers, bikers
    - May be provoked by high-pitched sounds
    - Dangerous
- **Protective aggression**
    - Protects human or humans from other humans or dogs
    - Moves between human and others
    - More aggressive behaviors likely to occur as distance decreases
    - Sometimes stimulated by quick movements or hugs
    - Not aggressive in absence of protected human(s)
- **Redirected aggression**
    - Occurs in response to a correction or thwarting of a behavior or desire
    - Victim was not part of the original social interaction
    - Part of the control complex that includes impulse-control aggression
- **Territorial aggression**
    - Protects property by barking, snarling, often by running a fence line (well-defined boundary of territory)
    - Intensifies as approach distance decreases
    - May quickly define new territory (car, kennel run)
    - May be part of the control complex that includes impulse-control aggression

Contrary to the claims of the whole "dominance theory" crowd, the most common cause of aggression is not that dogs are trying to take over the world. Rather, by far the type of aggression that I see most frequently in my practice is fear-related aggression. Conversations with other qualified professionals confirm that this is generally true for them as well. One of the reasons I do often offer a label for the aggressive behavior of the dog I'm working with is to replace the flawed "dominance aggression" label that someone else may have already given it. A frustrating number of clients come to me thinking their dog has "dominance aggression." When an owner perceives her dog as being "dominant" she mistakenly feels that she needs to exert herself to force the dog into submission. This is *always* (and I try to never say "always" or "never") *a grave mistake.*

CHAPTER 10

Fear Aggression

I never cease to be amazed by the number of my clients who have been told elsewhere that their dog is exhibiting "dominance aggression," when it's clear as the nose at the end of their dog's face that he's reacting out of fear. The first thing I do with these caring but misguided owners is help them see their dogs' aggression for what it is—a defensive response to protect themselves from the things that are frightening them.

President Franklin D. Roosevelt, speaking about the Great Depression, said "We have nothing to fear but fear itself." If only it were that simple when dealing with dog behavior instead of failing economies. Fear-related behaviors can be debilitating to the inappropriately fearful dog. They are heartbreaking, frustrating, even sometimes dangerous for the human trying to deal with her dog's strong emotional responses, and for the dog who may injure himself or others in his desperate efforts to escape or protect himself from the fear-causing stimulus.

Why dogs develop fear aggression

Dogs frequently aggress from fear due to a lack of adequate early socialization. While socialization is ongoing even after the primary early socialization period, and remedial socialization can repair some of the damage done by lack of early socialization, if a solid foundation isn't put in place during this critically important time, chances are good that the dog will be somewhat to significantly neophobic (fearful of new things) throughout his life.

Dogs can also become fearfully aggressive from bad experiences. A dog who is teased and tormented by humans may become aggressive in response, and may generalize his fear toward all humans, or toward the class of humans who abused him: children, men with beards, women wielding cleaning supplies, people in uniform, etc. A dog who has been attacked by another dog, or had a bad experience with another species—

cat, horse, cow—may become fearfully aggressive toward others of the species that frightened or injured him. A dog who is in pain can become fearful as a result of his anticipation of the pain.

A fearful dog's aggression begins as his natural response to whatever he perceives as threatening, and he becomes classically conditioned to have a negative association with that stimulus:

> "Other dogs are bad—they hurt me."
>
> "Cleaning ladies are bad—they carry scary things."
>
> "Children are bad—they poke things in my ears and pull my tail."
>
> "People using walkers are bad—they move funny."

When the dog has a strong emotional response to these classically conditioned aversive stimuli, he may growl, bark and/or lunge, even bite at the person or other animal to protect himself. In most cases, when a dog growls, barks or lunges, the scary thing goes away, and over time the dog becomes operantly conditioned—that is, he learns that he can make scary things go away, and he chooses to offer these aggressive behaviors deliberately in order to make the scary people go away.

Negative reinforcement, one of the four principles of operant conditioning, says "The dog's behavior makes a bad thing go away and, as a result, the behavior increases." (See The Four Principles of Operant Conditioning in Chapter 8.) Therefore, when a dog's aggressive behavior successfully makes scary people go away, his aggression is likely to increase. This is one reason you may see an adolescent dog initially offer low levels of distance-increasing "go away" behavior that escalates as he realizes the behavior works to make people go away. He has been reinforced for the behavior, so the behavior increases. What started as a natural, reflexive response ("Yikes! Go away, you scared me!") becomes conditioned through association ("Oh, I don't like people in uniforms—they are scary."), and the dog learns to operantly control the scary things ("Oh, I can make scary people in uniform go away by growling and barking at them, or even biting! I will growl, bark and bite faster, sooner, harder and stronger the next time!").

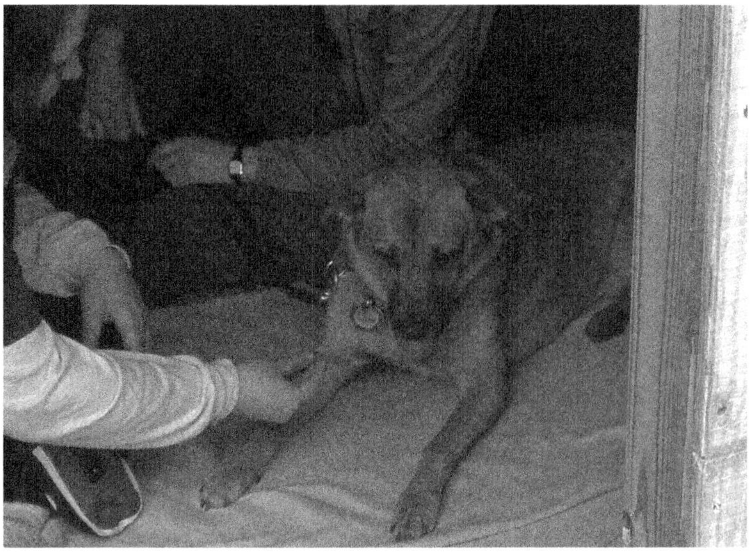

This dog is exhibiting fearful/shut down body language—her ears are back, she's turning her head away, and she is refusing the high-value treats that are being offered to her.

Because training methods that involve intimidation, coercion and physical force can cause undesirable side effects, including fear and aggression, positive trainers use primarily positive reinforcement, secondarily negative punishment, may carefully use negative reinforcement with the *sub-threshold* presentation of an aversive stimulus, and avoid the use of positive punishment. On those occasions where negative reinforcement may seem appropriate, it should be applied as gently as possible, avoiding a strong response from the dog—for example, teaching a dog to gently move away from pressure.

Three faces of fear

The complex of fear-related behaviors includes **fears, anxieties** and **phobias.** While they are closely related emotional responses, they differ significantly in several ways, including the presence or absence of an actual physical trigger, the intensity of the dog's response, and the ease with which the emotional response and related behaviors can be modified. In general, these three conditions can be among the most difficult of behavioral problems to treat.

Fears

There is a strong genetic component to fear-related behaviors. Whereas once we tended to place a lot of the blame on owners for their perceived role in creating fearful dogs, today we recognize that a genetic propensity toward fearfulness is a significant factor in the actual manifestation of fear-related behaviors. While environment—especially lack of socialization—can play a critically important role in bringing these behaviors to fruition, genes explain why two dogs with similar upbringing and socialization can react so differently in the presence of a potentially fear-causing stimulus, and why even a well-socialized dog can suddenly develop phobic behaviors.

Fear is defined as a feeling of apprehension associated with the actual presence or proximity of an object, individual or social situation perceived as a threat. It's a valuable, adaptive emotion, necessary for survival and appropriate in many situations. It's good to be afraid of grizzly bears, tornados and semi-trucks skidding out of control on icy highways. Your dog is wise to fear the flashing heels of a galloping horse, strong waves crashing on an ocean beach, the spinning wheels of a passing car. People and animals who feel no fear are destined to live short lives.

Of course, overly fearful dogs may lead short lives as well. Fear-related aggression is a significant risk to a dog's long and happy life. A fearful dog's first choice is usually to escape, but he may bite defensively if cornered or trapped, and dogs who bite are often euthanized. In addition, a constant emotional state of fear makes for a poor quality of life for a dog, and for humans who are stressed by their fearful dog's behavior.

Most biologists agree that human and nonhuman mammals experience fear similarly. Recall one of your own heart-stopping, adrenaline-pumping life experiences. Perhaps you were approached by a menacing stranger in an alley on a dark night, threatened by a large predator on a camping trip, cornered by an angry bull in a pasture, or just missed rear-ending a car in front of you when a moment of inattention caused you to miss the warning flash of taillights. Remember how helpless, vulnerable and terrified you felt? You can empathize with your dog when you see him trembling in the presence of a stimulus that elicits a similar response in his canine brain and body.

Anxieties

Anxiety is the distress or uneasiness of mind caused by apprehensive anticipation of pending danger or misfortune, real or imagined. Anxious dogs appear tense, braced for a threat they can't adequately predict, sometimes one that doesn't actually even exist. Anxiety can be a chronic condition, one that significantly impairs a dog's (and owner's) quality of life, and one that can be more challenging to modify than the fear of a real and present danger. Separation distress is perhaps the most widely discussed anxiety-related behavior in dogs, but owner absence is not the only cause for canine apprehension. Many dogs are anxious on car rides—anticipating, perhaps, a visit to the vet's office, or some other "bad" place. A dog who has been attacked by a loose dog while walking on leash may become anxious about going for walks, constantly stressed, scanning the neighborhood for another potential attacker.

Again, human anxieties are similar to canine. If you've been mugged in a dark alley, you are likely to experience some degree of stress anytime you find yourself walking down an alley in the dark. Some people experience extreme anxiety over taking exams, even when their past successes show that they pass tests with flying colors. Barbra

Streisand, successful singer that she is, suffers from extreme performance anxiety, still becoming physically ill every time she's about to walk on stage. The danger or misfortune may be imagined, but the anxiety is very real.

Phobias

Phobias are persistent, extreme, inappropriate fear or anxiety responses, far out of proportion to the level or nature of threat presented. They are stubbornly resistant to modification through habituation or desensitization—repeated low-level exposure to the stimulus that causes the extreme response. While inappropriate in degree, a phobic response is not totally irrational—it is usually directed toward something that could be harmful. Common human phobias are related to snakes, spiders, high places, flying—all things that have potential to be life threatening. In reality, the majority of snakes and spiders are relatively harmless, it's rare for humans to accidentally nosedive off a skyscraper, and only a tiny percentage of airplanes ever crash. Common canine phobias include extreme reactions to thunderstorms and other sounds, fear of humans and inappropriate response to novel stimuli (anything new and different).

Fear—the most common cause for aggressive behavior in dogs. This fearful dog could easily bite if the human foolishly persists in trying to touch him. Note the pinned-back ears and lowered body posture as the dog leans away from the human.

Getting brave

My go-to protocol for working with fears, phobias and anxieties is counter-conditioning and desensitization to change the dog's emotional response to the stimulus or situation, as described in Chapter 8. In her booklet, *The Cautious Canine,* author and behaviorist Dr. Patricia McConnell calls counter-conditioning a "universally effective treatment for fear-based behavior problems." Think of it as training your dog's emotions rather than training his actions. Behavior change will follow emotional change.

In addition to your counter-conditioning and desensitization work, there are a number of operant behaviors explained below that you can teach and utilize to help your dog better manage fear-causing encounters. Some of these involve **priming**—getting your dog's brain in a happy place to help him be better able to handle potentially distressing events. Again, think of your own experiences. If you are feeling good, and happy about life, and a distressing event occurs, you are emotionally far better able to deal with it than if you are already stressed and unhappy.

Basic good manners training

You don't always have to do a lot of fancy stuff to help your dog become more confident in his world. Simply teaching him basic good manners—to respond appropriately to your cues—will make his environment more predictable—he knows what you're asking of him, and he knows the consequences of his behavior. Of course it goes without saying that you will use positive reinforcement-based training with him so the consequences are happy ones. Nothing can destroy a fearful dog's confidence faster than the application of verbal or physical punishment by the very human he should be able to trust. That kind of treatment only serves to convince him he's right to think the world is a scary and unpredictable place.

Combine his positive reinforcement good manners training with structure in his routine and stability in his life and you will have taken a large step toward increasing his confidence. But, of course, you want to do more to help your dog get brave. Happily, you can do that simply by doing fun stuff with him. Read on...

Targeting

Targeting means teaching your dog to touch a designated body part to a designated target. That description doesn't do it justice...targeting is tons of fun! Many dogs love targeting, partly because it's easy to do, and partly because it pays off well—"push the button (the target spot), get a treat."

Since dogs naturally explore the world with their noses and paws, nose and foot targeting are the two easiest. Nose targeting draws your dog's eye contact and attention from a worrisome stimulus to a pleasant one, so that's the one I find most useful for timid dogs, although foot targeting can work too.

It's an embarrassingly simple behavior to teach. Hold out your hand in front of your dog, at his nose level or below. When he sniffs it (because he's curious!), click your clicker and feed him a treat (or use a verbal marker—a mouth click, or a word—and treat). Remove your hand, then offer it again. Each time he sniffs, click and treat. If he stops sniffing (boring—I've already sniffed that!) rub a little tasty treat smell on it, and try again.

You're looking for that wonderful "light bulb" moment—when he realizes he can make you click by bumping his nose into your hand. His "touch" behavior becomes deliberate, rather than incidental to the smells on your hand. When you see him deliberately bumping his nose into your hand, add the "Touch!" cue as you offer your hand to him. Encourage him with praise and high-value treats. Make it a game, so he thinks it's the most fun in the world. You want to see his eyes light up when you say "Touch," and you want him to "bonk" his nose into your hand, hard! Start offering your hand in different places so he has to move to touch it, climb on something to touch it, jump up to touch it.

When he loves the Touch game, occasionally ask him to touch twice, tell him he's a good dog after the first one, and only click and treat the second one. Gradually decrease your rate of reinforcement (but always give a treat when you click), until he'll touch several times before he gets his click and treat. Then click and treat several in a row. Mix it up, so he never knows when the click will happen (but the click and treat always happens eventually!).

Now try playing Touch when your dog's a little bit nervous about something. Scary man with a beard and sunglasses passing by on the sidewalk? Hold out your hand and say "Touch!" so your dog takes his eyes—and his brain—away from the scary thing and happily bonks his nose into your hand. Click and treat. Priming! He can't be afraid of the man and happy about touching your hand at the same time. He also can't look at your target hand and stare at the scary man at the same time.

After the Touch priming, revert to your counter-conditioning procedure until the man has passed, and then continue on your walk. By changing your dog's behavior—having him do something he loves rather than act fearful—you can set him up for more successful counter-conditioning, and eventually change his emotional response to an association with something previously scary to him. Eventually you should be able to drop the counter-conditioning and just play Touch until the man passes. Your dog is getting braver!

Targeting: a useful priming and management behavior—and a fun game for you and your dog.

Find It

Like targeting, "Find It" is a behavior many dogs learn to love, and another priming game you can play to change behavior in the presence of a fear-causing stimulus, eventually changing your dog's emotional response. This is also another ridiculously easy and delightful game that any dog can play.

Start with your dog in front of you, and handful of tasty treats behind your back. Say "Find it!" in a cheerful tone of voice and toss one treat a few feet to your left. When your dog gets to the treat, click just before he eats it. When he comes back to you say "Find it!" again and toss a second treat a few feet to your right. Click—and he eats the treat. Do this back and forth, until your dog is easily moving from one "Find It" treat to the other. Then toss them farther each time until your dog happily runs back and forth. Fun game!

Now if a scary skateboarder appears while you're walking your dog around the block on his leash, play Find It, keeping the tossed treats close to you. Your dog will take his eyes off the scary thing and switch into happy-treat mode. You've changed his emotions by changing his behavior.

Targeting and Find It can also work to walk your timid dog past a scary, stationary object, like a manhole cover or a noisy air conditioning unit. Touch-and-treat as you walk past, or toss Find It treats on the ground ahead of you and slightly away from the scary thing, to keep him moving happily forward.

Emergency Escape

Your Emergency Escape game gives you a "run away" strategy when you know an approaching stimulus will be too much for your worried dog. However, because you've taught it to your dog as a fun game, he's not running away in panic—he's just playing one of his favorite "Get Brave" games that just happens to move him farther away from the scary thing. Priming!

Teach this game to your dog in a safe, comfortable environment when he's not being afraid of something. As you are walking with him on leash, say your "Run Away!!" cue, then turn around and run fast, encouraging your dog to romp with you for a squeaky toy, a ball, a handful of high-value treats at the end of the run, or a rousing game of tug—whatever your dog loves. The key to success with this exercise is convincing your dog that the "Run Away" cue is the predictor of wonderful fun and games. Again—you're teaching him a new, fun behavior—Run Away!—that you can use to change his emotional response in a scary moment. He's getting braver.

Play

In fact, you can use any behavior your dog already loves—a trick, a toy, a game, anything that lights up his face—to convince him that good things happen in the presence of something scary. If he loves to roll over, ask him to do that. If he delights in snagging tossed treats out of the air, do that. High Five? Tug? Crawl? Spin and Twirl? Do those. You're priming!

They key to making any of these games work to help your dog be brave is to be sure you keep him far enough away from the scary thing, at first, that his brain is able to click into "play" mode. You will always be more successful if you start the games when you see low levels of stress, rather than waiting until he's in full meltdown. If he's too stressed or fearful, he won't be able to play. If he'll start to play games with you while the scary thing is at a distance, you'll be able to move closer. If he stops playing and shuts down, you've come too close. Depending on your dog and how fearful he is, you may find some of these play strategies work well enough to walk him past scary stimuli the first time you try, or you may have to work up to it.

You can use play as a primer both to put your dog in a happy frame of mind for his counter-conditioning work, and also as a barometer of his level of fear. If he is too stressed to play, he is over threshold. Reduce the intensity of the stimulus and try again.

Get Behind

"Get Behind" is more of a management strategy. Timid dogs often seek to hide when they are afraid. If you teach your dog a cue that means "hide behind me," your "body shield" can help him get through scary moments.

To teach this behavior:

1. Have your dog in front of you, with an ample supply of small, high-value treats in your treat pouch, or in a bowl on a nearby table.

2. Say "Get behind!" and lure your dog behind you and into a sit. Click and treat.

3. Repeat several times, until he lures easily into position.

4. Now say the cue and pause, to give him a chance to think about it and respond. If he moves even slightly, click, lure him into position, and treat. A tentative movement is sometimes a question to you—"Is this

what you want?" If you answer with a hearty "Click" (or "Yes!!") and treat, you can move the training forward more quickly.

5. Keep repeating the cue/pause, gradually reducing how much you lure, until he's moving into position on his own when you give the cue.

You can start applying this strategy in real-life situations early on in the training, even before your dog fully grasps the concept, simply by luring him into his safe position as the scary thing passes. Remember, however, that even with all of the games and management strategies, you must still protect your dog from scary things. It is critical to your success that you keep him under threshold as much as possible while you're implementing new strategies. If you force him to accept the attentions of bearded men while he is still fearful of them you can sensitize him to the scary stimuli, making his behavior worse instead of better.

Treat and Retreat

"Treat and Retreat" is a procedure that can be used to help timid dogs get brave. Its development is attributed to two well-known trainers: Dr. Ian Dunbar, veterinary behaviorist and founder of the Association of Professional Dog Trainers (*www.dogstardaily.com/training/retreat-amp-treat*), and Suzanne Clothier (*www.suzanneclothier.com*). While Dr. Dunbar claims credit for introducing the concept, Clothier is generally credited with popularizing the procedure under the "Treat and Retreat" phrase.

To use Treat and Retreat, start with your dog a safe distance from a person who worries him. As a safety precaution, have your dog on a long line so you can restrain him if necessary. Have the person toss a piece of low-value kibble over your dog's head. Your dog will turn and walk away to get the kibble, then turn back to look at the scary person. When he turns back, have the person toss a high-value treat in front of the dog, in the approximate place the dog was originally. (You will want to use some kind of marker to help your tossing person's aim.)

When the dog comes forward and eats the high-value treat, have the person toss another low-value treat behind the dog, then another high-value treat in the original spot. As your dog gets more relaxed about coming forward for the high-value treat, have the tosser gradually decrease the distance, so the dog is going closer to the scary person to eat the treat. If you see increased signs of reluctance with the decreased distance, you've decreased the distance too quickly. Go as slowly as necessary to keep your dog happy about this game—you want him moving toward the person tossing the treats happily and voluntarily.

Remember that aggression should not be taken lightly. If your dog acts aggressively or is so fearful it is impacting his (and your!) quality of life, your best option is to contact a qualified, positive behavior professional to help you decide which approach is best for you and your dog, and to help you implement it. You can also look for the book *Help For Your Fearful Dog* by Nicole Wilde. Be safe!

CHAPTER 11

Touch/Handling Sensitivity

At least dozens of times a day my hands are on my dogs. It might be to attach or untangle a leash, look into ears, check teeth, brush or trim fur in various places, put on a Thundershirt—a product that helps dogs (and cats) overcome their fears and anxieties using the gentle technique of maintained pressure, similar to the effect of swaddling for a human infant (*www.thundershirt.com*)—apply flea and tick preventative, or just to feel the soft, silky warmth of dog under my hand. We humans are a tactile species, and with our handy opposable thumbs, we're always doing something to manipulate our canine companions and their body parts.

Dogs, on the other hand aren't born with a natural love of being touched by humans. Dogs who have not been adequately socialized to accept the kinds of touch that they aren't innately fond of, or those who have had unpleasant experiences with a particular sort of handling, may resort to aggression to ward off further discomfort or express their displeasure at being touched. They have to learn that human touch is good. A well-socialized puppy learns early in life that human hands make good things happen, and many dogs love being touched by us as much as we love touching them. When I sit on the sofa in the evenings typing on my laptop, Bonnie, our 11-year-old Scorgidoodle, is snuggled close on my right side, while our Kelpie, Kai, is curled up on my left. Both of them love being petted. Our 12-year-old Cardigan Corgi, Lucy, and 13-year-old Pomeranian, Scooter, however, will lie nearby but not touching me—they are not as thrilled by close contact.

Scooter, the author's Pomeranian, is not a cuddler. He is generally comfortable being touched, but is not fond of being groomed. Fortunately, he has great bite inhibition, despite this alarming display in response here to the comb in Pat Miller's hand.

Hands on

As listed above, there are countless legitimate reasons to touch your dog. Part of a good puppy socialization program involves convincing your young dog that human touch is a wonderful thing. This is classical conditioning—giving your pup a good association with touch (and with all the other things he's likely to encounter in his lifetime). A well-socialized pup is an optimist, believing that the world is a good place, and new things are safe unless and until proven otherwise. Getting your dog to accept new things throughout his life like Thundershirts, Calming Caps (products designed/intended to help your dog stay calm), nail clippers, stethoscopes and otoscopes is much easier if he is well-socialized.

Counter-conditioning is the process of changing your dog's existing association with something—usually from negative to positive. If someone at some time in your dog's life made the mistake of muzzling him and forcibly holding him down while clipping his nails, your dog now thinks nail trimming can be a terrifying ordeal, and is willing to bite to protect himself. You can use counter-conditioning to convince him, instead, that nail trimming is a wonderful thing, by pairing bits and pieces of the nail trimming process with high-value treats, and gradually putting the whole process together.

You are working to convince your dog that nail trimming makes really good stuff happen. But that's not all you can do. With many husbandry procedures that are problematic for some dogs, you can invite your dog to willingly participate in the process.

Our Corgi, Lucy, isn't fond of nail trimming. It's mostly the paw-restraint part she objects to. So I taught her to lie on the floor, paws extended so I can reach her nails with the clippers and trim nails without ever having to hold her paws. Many treats accompany the process, but we can accomplish nail trimming without a struggle.

Hands off

Whenever possible, invite your dog to voluntarily offer a behavior rather than trying to physically manipulate him—as described above with Lucy's nail trimming. This can save you a lot of resistance, aggression and heartache. I *never* attempt to pull my dog out of a crate, off the bed or sofa (yes, my dogs are allowed on the furniture) or otherwise move them—except for occasional gentle pressure with a leash when appropriate. Rather, I teach them an "Off" or "Out" cue, ask them to target to my hand, or if necessary toss treats to get them to voluntarily move when and where I need them to, especially if they are reluctant to do so. To teach "Off," invite your dog up on the sofa, say "Off!" and toss a treat on the floor. Repeat until your dog jumps off the sofa when you say "Off," in anticipation of the coming treat. To teach "Out," invite your dog into his crate, then say "Out" and toss a treat far enough away from the crate that he has to come out to get it. Repeat until your dog emerges from the crate when you say "Out," in anticipation of the coming treat.

Choices

We humans tend to be happier with our lives when we can make our own choices. So do our dogs. The better we are at giving them choice opportunities and setting them up to want to make the right choices, the happier we both are. If you can convince your dog to willingly and happily choose to participate in a husbandry procedure, everyone is better off. When your dog is a happy, willing participant, it is highly unlikely he will feel the need to bite. Another alternative to the above-described counter-conditioning for nail trimming is to provide your dog with a canine-sized emery board, teach him to use it, and let him choose to file his own nails. (Note: Some owners report that their dogs love to file their own nails so much that they have to put the board away or their dogs file their nails down to the bloody quick.)

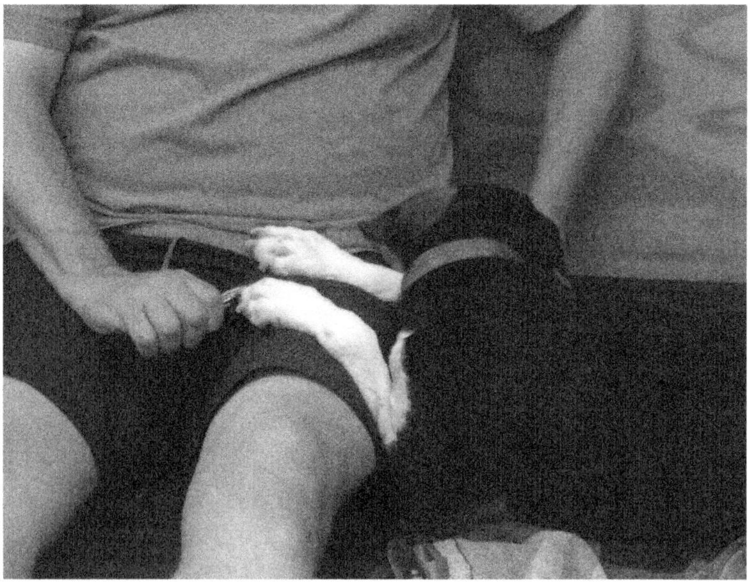

Nail trimming without restraint—expose nails by having dog lie down with paws on floor, or on a raised surface such as your leg. Then trim—with lots of treats for a positive association.

Or teach your dog to file his own nails on a canine emery board!

Let's look at some different handling challenges and see how we can use both counter-conditioning and choice in step-by-step protocols to make life much safer and far less stressful for all concerned. Whatever procedure(s) you use, you can set your dog up for success by priming before you begin. As mentioned above, priming is a behavioral effect in which exposure to a stimulus your dog loves (ball, tug) influences a response to a later stimulus that he doesn't love (child, skateboard, being touched). While well-documented in human behavior, the concept of priming is less well-known in the world of dog training and behavior. Simply put, if you prime your dog with tasty treats or a fun activity prior to engaging in the handling activity, your dog is in a happier frame of mind to begin the procedure, and thus better able to make choices and respond from a less stressful place.

With the following procedures, know that they will take longer, and you will generally need to move forward more slowly (and carefully!), if your dog already has a negative association with the procedure, and especially if he has shown signs of aggression during the procedure.

Wiping muddy feet

Classical conditioning: For all classical conditioning procedures, do multiple repetitions of each step, feeding a high-value treat—I like to use chicken—after each repetition. Only move to the next step when your dog gets happy at the previous step, letting you know he's made the association between the procedure and the high-value treat. If he seems uncomfortable at any step, back up to the previous step until he's happy again, and then figure out a smaller, intermediate step. An intermediate step between Step 1 and Step 2 below might be to put pressure on the foot but not pick it up. If he's not even comfortable having his foot touched, start by touching his elbow or shoulder, and slowly work your way down. Remember that for proper classical conditioning, you present the stimulus first (i.e., touch the foot) and *then* present the food. You want him to think that the touch makes the treat appear.

1. Touch foot with your hand, feed.
2. Rest foot on your hand without holding it, feed.
3. Hold foot with your hand (a few seconds at first, then gradually longer), feed.
4. Towel in your hand, feed.
5. Touch towel to foot, feed.
6. Touch towel to foot while foot is held in your hand, feed.
7. Rub foot gently with towel, feed.
8. Rub foot more vigorously with towel, feed.

Choice: (make the training process rewarding enough that your dog will happily choose to offer the behaviors when you ask for them):

1. Train your dog to walk through a plastic tub with water in it (start with an empty tub and add water gradually if your dog is worried about the water). Use shaping (reinforce small approximations/pieces of the behavior, gradually working your way to the full behavior) or luring, or a combination of both.

2. Teach your dog to stand on an absorbent mat or towel to wick off the water.

3. Alternatively, shape your dog to actually wipe his feet on the absorbent mat or towel to hasten the drying process.

4. Put the behavior on cue so you can invite your dog to choose to perform the desired behavior. If you have trained your dog well, he will happily choose to offer the behavior when you ask.

Lifting

Classical conditioning:

1. Place both hands briefly, gently, on either side of your dog's spine, feed.

2. Gradually move your hand down and under your dog's ribcage on the far side, touching and feeding multiple times at each step.

3. Gradually move your other hand around the front of your dog's chest to his shoulder opposite you, touching and feeding multiple times at each step.

4. Put light pressure on your dog with both hands, gradually hugging him toward you, feed.

5. Gradually increase pressure, feeding multiple times at each step.

6. Hugging your dog against your chest, lift upward slightly, release and feed.

7. Gradually increase the amount of lift pressure until you are picking him up, feeding multiple times at each step.

(Note: Be careful with this one. When you lift, your fearful dog's face will be near yours. Injured dogs especially are very likely to bite if you try to lift them, because they are in pain. Whenever possible, *avoid* lifting a dog unless and until you are confident he is very comfortable with it. It is always advisable to muzzle an injured dog prior to lifting.)

Choice #1, small dog:

1. Shape or lure-shape your dog to go into a carrier on cue.
2. Lift the carrier to transport your dog to the desired location.
3. Treat while carrier is being carried, to offset any negative association with the movement of the carrier.
4. Treat when you place the carrier at the destination, again to maintain a positive association with the moving process.

Choice #2, small to medium-sized dog:

1. Shape or lure-shape your dog to jump into your lap when you are seated on the floor. Put the behavior on cue.
2. Make a circle of your arms in your lap so when he jumps into your lap he is jumping into your arms. Practice until the behavior is fluent (happens quickly and easily) and on cue.
3. Kneel, and cue him to jump into your arms. Practice until fluent.
4. Sit in a chair and cue him to jump into your arms. Practice until fluent.
5. Stand and cue him to jump into your arms. Be sure you catch him!

Choice #3, any size dog:

1. Purchase a portable ramp or steps made for dogs.
2. Shape or lure-shape your dog to walk up the ramp or the steps. Put it on cue.
3. Practice until the behavior is fluent.
4. Use the ramp or steps in place of picking him up when you need him on an elevated surface such as getting into the back of your SUV or onto the exam table at your veterinarian's office.

Some behaviors don't lend themselves well to a total choice approach, but you may be able to use a choice/conditioning hybrid procedure, still giving your dog some sense of control over his own world—and you can still give your dog the choice to participate—or not. Here's one such procedure:

Putting on a harness (jacket, Thundershirt, etc.)

Classical conditioning:

1. Hold up the harness with one hand, feed.
2. Let him sniff or nose-touch the harness, feed.
3. Let him sniff the harness and feed treats through the opening that will go over his head.
4. Let him sniff the harness, and feed treats farther away so he has to move his head farther into the harness.
5. Rest the harness on his neck, feed.
6. Reach toward the strap that buckles, feed. (Note: you can smear peanut butter or squeeze cheese on your refrigerator door for him to lick, to keep him occupied while you fasten the buckles.)
7. Touch the strap that buckles, feed.
8. Move the strap that buckles, feed.
9. Touch the strap that buckles to the strap it buckles into, feed.
10. Snap the buckle closed, feed. (Note—if your dog is sound sensitive you might choose to counter-condition the sound of the buckle snapping closed first, or the Velcro sound of the Thundershirt, prior to and separate from the procedure of putting the harness on the dog.)

Choice and classical conditioning:

1. Shape your dog to walk into the harness, suspended from something (a table, a sawhorse, etc.) to give him access. Click and treat as he offers to move incrementally farther into the suspended harness.
2. When he is voluntarily moving into the harness, use classical conditioning Steps 6 through 10 above to complete the process.

Even behaviors that don't lend themselves well to choice, such as trimming hair and medicating ears, can incorporate an element of choice (and priming), by teaching your dog to station—to go to a specific spot where nine times out of ten (or better yet, 99 times out of 100), really good, fun stuff happens. If, every once in a great while, a slightly less-fun (but not hugely aversive) procedure happens, it shouldn't be enough to change his happy association with his station, especially if you do much of the classical conditioning away from the station, and only invite him to station when he has a positive association with all the parts of the procedure. Remember, multiple repetitions at every step until the dog is happy!

Trimming hair over eyes (on legs, etc.)

1. Show your dog the scissors, feed. (Use blunt-end scissors until your dog is very comfortable with the procedure.
2. Move scissors toward dog, feed.
3. Let him sniff the scissors, feed.
4. Move scissors as if you were cutting, several inches from dog, feed.
5. Move scissors toward neck, feed.
6. Touch scissors to neck, feed.
7. With scissors close to neck, move scissors as if cutting, feed.
8. Touch scissors next to eye, feed.
9. With scissors near eyes, move scissors as if cutting, feed.
10. Add other parts of the trimming procedure that might be specific to your dog (combing the hair, holding a lock of hair with one hand, etc.) feed.
11. Snip one piece of hair, feed.
12. Gradually increase the number of hair snips, feed.
13. Now move the procedure to the station to add in a small element of choice.

I could go on forever. There are countless procedures that involve touching and handling our dogs, and each could be spelled out in a protocol that uses choice, classical conditioning, or a combination of the two, to make life easier for both you and your dog. But I bet by now you've got the idea. Whether your challenge is applying topical flea and tick preventative, cleaning and/or putting medication in ears, grooming, flea combing, brushing teeth, pulling ticks, or whatever, you are always far better off figuring out how to help your dog become a willing partner in the activity rather than restraining and coercing him into accepting the procedure. Every time you use physical coercion or manipulation, you increase the chances for aggression. Unless it's a medical emergency, there's no need to use force. Wouldn't you rather have choices?

CHAPTER 12

Predatory Aggression

Dogs can exhibit predatory behavior toward other domestic animals (including small dogs!) as well as wildlife. It is a natural, normal food-acquiring behavior for canines (albeit one frowned upon by many dog owners), and not truly classified as aggression, although the end result to the victim may be the same. This doesn't mean it's not serious. Some human fatalities, especially where the victim is an infant, are believed to be a result of predatory behavior. Management, in conjunction with the counter-conditioning process described in the following case history, can effectively control and modify some predatory behavior. Still, many dogs who live in perfect harmony with cats indoors have been known to chase and kill free-roaming outdoor cats.

A dog and cats tale

Ken and Susan Johnson love German Shepherds and are very aware of the pet over-population problem. So it made sense, when their senior Shepherd died of old age, to adopt their next canine companion from a rescue group. They contacted a German Shepherd rescue and adopted five-year-old black-and-tan Sara. The rescue told them that Sara, seized in a neglect case, had lived with cats in her previous home, so they felt confident taking her home to meet their senior cat. Much to their dismay, they discovered that while Sara may have lived with cats before, it probably wasn't a harmonious relationship. When we met for our first behavior modification session they said, "We had a cat when we first brought Sara home. She chased the cat upstairs where he stayed for the next two months until he passed away of natural causes."

Sara, dedicated to chasing cats, with serious intent to do harm.

Ken and Susan also love cats, and were aching to adopt a bonded pair to fill the void left by their last cat's passing. Wisely, however, they didn't want to subject two new cats to constant harassment by an aroused dog dedicated to committing feline mayhem. They asked if I could help Sara learn to get along with cats. I said we could try, and they signed up for a series of private behavior modification consults. The Johnsons were committed to keeping Sara whether we succeeded or not. They *really* wanted cats in their home, but were prepared to remain catless if we couldn't make it work.

Enter Barney

We have three cats in the Miller household. Although they live with our own four dogs, I knew that Blue and Viva wouldn't take kindly to participating in behavior modification sessions with a rowdy German Shepherd. Barney, however, is unflappable, and thus was drafted to be our "neutral cat."

On the day of the Johnsons' first scheduled session in mid-December of 2012, I brought Barney out to the training center and placed him in a covered exercise pen, with a blanket over the top so he couldn't leap out. We wanted him confined for his own safety, as well as to minimize his movement to help keep Sara's arousal level low. I put an open carrier inside so Barney had a place to hide if he felt threatened by Sara. The stage was set. We were just waiting for the Johnsons to arrive.

Cross-species relationships

While canines and felines are notorious for "fighting like cats and dogs," they are not the only potential "mixed-family" challenge. Dogs not well-socialized to other species can pose a threat to many other companion animals, from small rodents to rabbits, fish, birds, ferrets, pigs, goats, sheep, horses and everything in between.

My modification protocol of choice for introducing a dog to a new species is classical conditioning—giving the dog a positive association with the new creature, while at the same time managing (leash, crate, baby gate, closed door, etc.) so said dog never learns the joy of chasing said [insert your species of choice here] in your home. Because classical and operant conditioning are working together all the time, at the same time your dog is creating a healthy association with your new furred, finned or feathered family member (cockatiels make chicken happen!) he is also learning a new behavior (if I sit by my human's side when cockatiel is present I can make her feed me chicken). If you're proactive with your introductions—and if your dog didn't come to you with already-installed chase-other-animals associations, you can often create harmony in your household in a short time with reasonable effort.

If, however, you have a dog like Sara who already has an unhealthy predator/prey or other negative association with other species, you'll have to work hard to counter-condition and desensitize her association and related behavior.

Counter-conditioning Sara—Session 1

The Johnsons arrived for their scheduled appointment, and after a brief discussion about the plan, we set to work. We initially introduced Sara to Barney-in-the-pen at a distance of 40 feet. I find that to be a good average threshold distance for most of my clients' dogs in the presence of their arousal-causing stimuli. Not Sara! When she saw a cat 40 feet away she was immediately over threshold—ignoring food (venison instead of chicken, due to Sara's food allergies), whining and aroused, trying to drag Susan toward the pen.

We backed up to 60 feet and tried again. At this increased distance Sara was able to begin working, and quickly made the association between Barney and venison. Before long she was looking at Barney and quickly looking back to Ken for her treat. This swift development of a CER (conditioned emotional response) gave us hope for success, despite her initial intense reaction to cat-in-pen. By the end of the session, Sara was able to be within 25 feet of Barney's pen with relaxed, soft body language and expression. Since the Johnsons didn't have access to an accommodating Barney-style cat at home, I sent them off for two weeks to practice counter-conditioning Sara to the squirrels in her neighborhood—another source of high arousal for their dog.

Sara—Session 2

Improvement at the next session was slow but obvious. We started this session at a distance of 50 feet and ended 20 feet away from Barney in his pen. For the most part, Sara was far more interested in Ken and the venison than she was in Barney. We incorporated Leslie McDevitt's "Look at That" (LAT) exercise that teaches a dog to look at a stimulus on cue, so we could operantly cue Sara to look at Barney in order to get treats and continue strengthening the association between cat and venison. (See McDevitt's book, *Control Unleashed* for more information on her "Look at That" exercise.)

We added in "relax" sessions, moving 60 feet away from Barney and asking Sara to lie quietly at Ken and Susan's feet. We continued to feed venison if she looked at Barney, but also reinforced her just for settling and relaxing. We wanted her to understand she could just "hang" in the vicinity of a cat without always expecting treat action. Susan reported that Sara was becoming much less aroused when she saw squirrels on their walks. I suggested the Johnsons purchase a realistic-looking "Melissa and Doug" stuffed cat so they could practice these exercises with Sara in their home, in addition to their work with squirrels.

Sara had also been diagnosed with hypothyroidism and was on medication for this condition. The adjustment to her thyroid levels was doubtless contributing to her behavioral improvement.

Sara—Session 3

At Session 3 we were able to close the distance to 25 feet, getting good CERs, using the LAT cue to get Sara to look at Barney when needed, and interspersing "relax" periods in between the counter-conditioning work. This session we taught Sara an operant "Find It!" exercise, so we would have a tool to refocus her if she appeared close to threshold.

Sara—Session 4-5

Sara continued to show marked improvement. We closed the distance to two feet, with Ken sitting on the floor between dog and cat and petting them both. As proof that Sara was becoming non-threatening, Barney moved freely around his pen and even reached through the wires toward Ken. This sparked a little interest from Sara, but didn't send her over threshold.

As he was sitting on the floor between Sara and Barney, Ken looked at me and said quietly, "I never thought we would be able to do this." His heartfelt comment brought tears to my eyes.

Time for a serious discussion about where to proceed from here. I had begun reaching out to all my trainer contacts, looking for a bonded pair of cats who were in need of a home, and who grew up with dogs, so they wouldn't be put off by a dog who might become over-excited by their presence. We scheduled our next session at the Johnson home—Barney would be going on a field trip so Sara could practice her newly found calm skills in the presence of a cat in her own home.

Sara—Session 6-10

We did five sessions with Barney in the Johnson home. Sara was, indeed, aroused at the first introduction. The Johnson house is significantly smaller than our training center, and we could only work at a maximum line-of-sight distance of about 20 feet. We set Barney's pen up near the front door, by the stairs, and brought Sara in from the back yard.

Sara heard Barney meow before she saw him, and was instantly excited, whining and pulling toward the sound. Ken fed her until she calmed, and we moved her into view of Barney. With continued counter-conditioning it took about 20 minutes for her to settle on her bed. We started implementing the Karen Overall Protocol for Relaxation—a procedure that teaches a dog to remain calm while the owner very gradually moves away from the dog. We didn't want Sara to have to be right next to Ken and Susan the entire time cats were in the house. We also practiced "Relax," encouraging Sara to lie calmly on her side with her head down.

Session 10 was in mid-April, four months after we initially started working with Sara. She was now able to remain quite calm with Barney moving around freely in the pen. At this session we again had Ken sitting on the floor between dog and cat, and decided to risk going one step further and allow Sara to sniff Barney.

Sara greeted Barney calmly and politely, but to our surprise and dismay, Barney reacted with a loud hiss, and swatted Sara on the nose. Happily, Sara took the reprimand calmly, without any sign of arousal. She had just graduated from get-along-with-cat school—with honors. Ken, Susan and I looked at each other, delighted and amazed.

"She's as ready as she'll ever be," I said. Ken nodded.

I had recently located a trainer with a pair of cats who sounded like they met our needs perfectly.

"I'll call Jessi," Ken said.

Cats in the Johnson home

Ken and Susan met with Jessi and the two longhaired black cat brothers, Ralphie and Randy—and brought them home. We had agreed that the cats would stay safely stashed in a bedroom until our next session, when I could help with the introduction.

Ralphie and Randy move into the Johnson home.

A week later I arrived for the big moment. Ken and Susan had been letting the cats roam the house whenever Sara was in the back yard, so she was familiar with their scent, and the cats made plenty of noise as they romped together in their bedroom, so she had heard them playing. We placed Ralphie and Randy in the exercise pen that the Johnsons had purchased, and we brought Sara in.

Sara was curious but calm, and began offering CERs in less than three minutes. She easily went and lay down on her bed on cue, and didn't become aroused when Ralphie and Randy started to wrestle on their cat tree. After a 30-minute session of CERs and relaxation, we invited Randy and Ralphie back upstairs to their bedroom and breathed a collective sigh of relief. All was going according to plan.

Satisfying results of properly done counter-conditioning and desensitization.

I had one prepaid session left with the Johnsons. The plan was for them to continue controlled interaction daily between Sara and the cats for a couple of weeks—more concentrated now that they had their own cooperative cats to work with. However, changes in my schedule interfered, and it was a full month before I could come back for our final session at the end of May. I called the day before to confirm our appointment.

"How are things going?" I asked Susan when she answered the phone.

"We have an integrated household!" she exclaimed happily.

Although the plan had been to not allow free interaction until I was there to assist, Ralphie, the bolder of the cat brothers, had other ideas. Several days before my scheduled visit he made a break for the bedroom door when Susan went in to feed him, and dashed down the stairs to the living room where Sara was resting. It was a non-event. Sara calmly watched Ralphie dash past. All the Johnsons' hard work had paid off in spades. When I arrived for our final session all we had to do was sit and smile as we watched Sara, Ralphie and Randy amicably sharing their living space.

A happily blended Johnson family.

Beyond cats

The same counter-conditioning technique that worked for Sara, Ralphie and Randy can work equally well for conditioning your dog to get along with other species. A lot of our clients' dogs are startled to meet horses for the first time when they come to our property, and react to these monster-sized aliens (to them) by barking, even lunging at them. After a few "horses-make-chicken-happen" associations, most dogs behave appropriately around the horses, seeing them as a source of chicken rather than as threat or prey. I've even successfully counter-conditioned a dog who had an unhealthy intensity about fish in an aquarium to live peacefully with his aquatic family members.

The Johnsons were successful integrating cats into their home with the previously cat-reactive Sara for several reasons. Attention to these same factors will increase your likelihood of success regardless of what other species you might want to introduce into your household:

- **Short-term management:** The Johnsons managed Sara's environment so she wasn't regularly reinforced for chasing cats or other small animals. Behaviors that are reinforced repeat and increase. It is well-nigh impossible to modify an unwanted behavior if the dog is allowed to repeatedly practice the behavior and be reinforced for it. Whether fish, feline, fowl, ferret or other small companion animal, keeping your new family members safely isolated from your dog when not under your direct supervision is key to success—unless and until you are 100 percent sure your dog will do them no harm. With large animals such as livestock, management for safety goes both ways. As much as your dog can injure or even kill a horse or cow, he can also be badly injured or killed by them. Manage, manage, manage, until you are confident that things will go well.

- **Long-term management:** It was too soon at first to know if Sara would ever be able to be trusted home alone with Ralphie and Randy. The signs were promising, and as long as all continued to go well, the Johnsons intended to start a program of gradual departures—for just a couple of minutes at first, and then adding a few minutes at time. If Sara at any time showed any indication of a return to her prior aroused behavior around the cats, then management would be long term, with dog and cats never left alone together when their humans weren't home to intervene if needed. You will need to make the same judgment for your own multi-species household.
- **Commitment:** The Johnsons were serious about their goal of adopting cats into their family, and were willing to commit their time, energy and other resources to making it happen. I have many clients who are seriously committed to implementing the modification protocols we create, and I was still impressed by the Johnsons' investment in helping Sara learn to accept cats in her home. It may not take as much time and energy if your dog is less intense about other animals than Sara, but you still need to be prepared to do what it takes to make it work.
- **Realistic expectations:** The Johnsons knew they would need to find behaviorally compatible cats. They were willing to wait until they could find the right cats, and until Sara was ready for cats to come into the home. Cats who were likely to be stressed by an intense dog would not have been a wise choice, nor would it have been smart—or fair—to rush things and introduce cats too soon in the process. Ken and Susan knew they were taking on a major project, and were prepared to give up their dream of adopting cats if we weren't successful in our behavior modification program.
- **Prior history:** The Johnsons were flying a little blind on this one. Although Sara reportedly had lived in harmony with cats in a prior home, her behavior didn't support that statement. In fact, it appeared more likely that she *hadn't*. Predatory behavior alone isn't an automatic rule out—the Miller dogs have killed groundhogs here on our farm, and still live quite happily with our three house cats. However, if your dog has a strong reinforcement history for extremely inappropriate behavior toward other species—if he has successfully *killed* cats, or other domestic animals, it may be a huge challenge to bring potential prey into your home—and perhaps unfair to the potential victims. Think long and hard about how well you can manage your environment, and how committed you are to doing the work to modify the behavior. One management slip could be fatal.

Follow up

I originally worked with the Johnsons and Sara in the winter/spring of 2013. I recently contacted them (early in 2016) to see how things were going. Sara is now completely relaxed and trustworthy with Ralphie and Randy. The cats like her, sometimes curling up on her bed with her. Randy stands up on his hind legs and gives Sara head butts, which she tolerates quite nicely. All is calm in the Johnson household.

Good news

The good news is that many dogs can and do live peacefully with other species. It happens day in and day out, all over the world. With a little luck your dog has no prior unhealthy association with the "other" of your choice, and you can plan to do a minimal classical conditioning program to get your housemates off together on the right paw, wing or fin. If you end up with a Sara, you may need to find a good, positive reinforcement–based behavior professional to help you, but there's still a good chance you can make things work. Choose carefully, manage well, make the commitment and be realistic. *(Remember: Many dogs live quite peacefully with prey species in their own homes, but will chase and even catch and kill the same species outside.)*

Here's to your happily blended multi-species household!

CHAPTER 13

Resource Guarding: Dog-Human

The term "resource guarding" sends a chill through behavior professionals who understand that the aggression a dog displays when guarding a valuable resource, including food, toys, valued resting places or even beloved family members, can mean a death sentence for that dog, especially if the guarding occurs during a behavioral assessment of a dog in a shelter or rescue. But should it? There is a growing body of evidence that perhaps we've been overreacting all these years.

Resource guarding is, in fact, a natural, normal behavior, and an important survival strategy. For a wild animal, loss of important resources can mean death. Dogs do it. Cats do it. Horses do it—and so do a lot of other species. Even humans do it. Do you lock your car doors when you park on a city street? You are resource guarding. Do you lock your house when you leave for work in the morning, or head out for a shopping trip? You are resource guarding. If you try to sneak a bite off my plate while I'm eating my beloved pumpkin pie, I might just stab you with my fork. That's resource guarding. So how did a natural, normal behavior come to be so demonized that countless dogs have lost their lives as a result?

Scooter's hard eye, intense expression and position hovered over the object suggest he is not willing to share his toy. These somewhat subtle signals can be easy to miss for an unaware observer.

Stay away from my food! This dog's signals are more obvious—ears pinned back, whale eye, teeth bared, with the corners of the mouth pulled forward in an offensive/aggressive "C" shape. This message would be hard to miss!

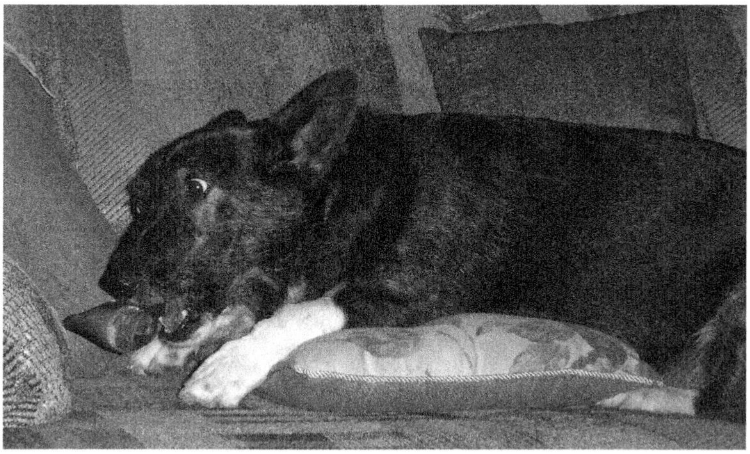

In contrast, while it's easy to mistake this for resource guarding because of the whale eye, note that Lucy is behind the vertical, her ears are back but not pinned back, and she's not protecting her toy. She's playing!

Prior to the 1990s, behavior assessments were conducted at shelters on a haphazard basis, if at all. At the time, when some 18 million homeless dogs and cats were euthanized at shelters annually, any presentation of aggression, including resource guarding, was enough reason to land a dog on the euthanasia list. As spay and neuter efforts and other education programs became increasingly effective, shelter numbers started to decline, and animal protection professionals were able to make more thoughtful and measured decisions through more standardized assessment processes. Still, the often dramatic responses dogs can offer when protecting their valuables continued to make it highly likely that a dog who guarded was selected for euthanasia. And since "resource guarding" had a bad name as an easily-identifiable trigger for aggression, even less intense guarding responses were still likely to result in the dog's death.

As animal protection professionals became convinced of the value and importance of assessing adoption dogs in order to ensure public safety, it seemed logical to refrain from placing dogs who demonstrated overt, identifiable aggressive behaviors, including guarding. The overreaction—euthanasia of all dogs who displayed any signs of resource guarding—stemmed from a well-meaning desire to not put adopters at risk. But it was, in fact, an overreaction.

For eight years, I volunteered at the nearby Humane Society of Washington County. We assessed dogs using a modified version of a protocol developed by Kelley Bollen for her master's thesis. Bollen's protocol was a modified version of Sue Sternberg's (Sternberg was one of the pioneers of the concept of behavior evaluations for shelter dogs), and also included the resource guarding test. When I started volunteering there in 2004, any sign of resource guarding resulted in euthanasia for the dog. By the time I left in 2012, we had created a continuum of outcomes for dogs with guarding behavior, and only the most extreme cases were euthanized. Other options included careful placement in an experienced home without small children, behavior modification work in a foster home prior to placement, and transfer to a rescue group with the resources to manage and modify the behavior. Of course, each shelter and rescue organization has its own tolerance for risk, and has to make its own decisions about what level of guarding they feel is suitable for placement.

Shares Well ←———|———→ **Guards Resource**

SHARES WELL:

Shares: Interested in food or object, but will readily and happily give it up.

¾ Shares: Continues eating with no signs of uneasiness; mild resistance to giving up object.

½ Shares: Continues eating; mild resistance to giving up object or food.

¼ Shares: Some tension with food bowl or object; eats faster; resists giving or tries to leave with object.

MIDDLE: Moves muzzle deeper into bowl; resists giving up object.

GUARDS RESOURCE:

¼ Guards: Freeze; low growl; does not move head toward hand.

½ Guards: Tension; freeze; whale eye; growl; moves head toward hand.

¾ Guards: Growl; freeze; whale eye; snap. (Candidate for breed rescue)

Guards: Bites. Responds with strong aggression. (Euthanasia)

Managing guarding behavior

Three of my four current dogs (all adopted from shelters or rescue) will easily guard resources, from both humans and from other dogs. Because we have no small children in the home, and because my husband, Paul, and I are reasonably knowledgeable and capable canine caretakers, we choose to mostly manage rather than modify our dogs' behaviors. Management includes feeding Scooter, our Pomeranian, in a separate room with the door closed, and monitoring the other three while they eat; separating dogs to give them high-value chews using crates, baby gates and closed doors; and always asking them to trade for a treat when we need to take something from them, rather than trying to grab it from their mouths—a good idea even if your dog doesn't guard.

If you are considering the management option for your resource guarder, critically evaluate your home environment to determine if management is truly a realistic long-term solution.

Here are some of the factors that would suggest modification might be needed as well as management:

- Children live in or regularly visit the home.
- One of more adults living in the home will not dependably adhere to management protocols.
- Dog's guarding behavior is fierce and unpredictable (will guard random dropped/found objects, not just food).

If you decide that modification is needed, remember that at least for the short term you will need to put stringent management measures in place. While management always carries the possibility of failure, the more you do to reduce that possibility, the safer all will be.

Modifying guarding behavior

Dogs guard resources because they fear losing them. Sometimes the fear is learned through experience—someone has been taking valuable resources away from the dog. Some silly humans seem to think they have an absolute right to take anything away from their dogs at any time, and their dogs should let them, without protest. That's a terrific way to create a resource guarding behavior. It's rude to grab something from someone. We learned that in kindergarten, right? I would no more rudely grab something from a dog than I would from another human. Other dogs are guardy from a very early age, even absent known encounters with rude resource-grabbing humans. Even six-to eight-week-old puppies can show resource guarding behavior—to their littermates and to humans.

Either way, your goal is to convince your dog that a human approaching him when he is in possession of a resource is not a threat to his resource, but rather predicts the arrival of more good stuff. Caveat: If your dog has caused serious injury to a person or another animal, or you are not comfortable implementing this protocol on your own, please seek the assistance of a qualified force-free behavior professional!

Teaching "Trade"

"Trade" is a useful behavior for non-guarders as well as dogs who guard their valuables. If you are teaching this to a dog who guards, be *extra-cautious* not to pressure him, start the game with very low-value objects, and be quick to resort to a "Hansel and Gretel Trail" if you see any sign of tension during the "Trade" game.

Here's how to play "Trade":

1. Offer your dog a well-stuffed KONG or other favorite toy (lower value if your dog guards) and say "Take it!" Have him on a leash if you think he'll run off with it.

2. Give him a little while to get fully engaged in chewing, and then say "Trade!" in a cheerful tone of voice and offer him a handful of irresistible treats, such as small bits of chicken or low-fat cheese.

3. Hold the treats near his nose and let him sniff. It may take him several seconds for him to think about it, but eventually he should drop his toy and start eating the treats. Don't let him eat them in one gulp! Protect the tidbits in your hand a little so he can only nibble them one by one.

4. When he drops the toy, say "Yes!"

5. While he is still nibbling treats out of your treat hand, reach down with your other hand and pick up the chew toy.

6. Let him nibble a bit longer, then offer him the toy again.

Repeat the exercise several times, then end the game by giving him back his toy and letting him chew to his heart's content. Play this game at every opportunity, whenever he's engaged in chewing on his toys on his own, or whenever you feel like initiating the game, until he'll give up his chew object easily on your "Trade" cue.

The "Trade" game doesn't always go as smoothly as you might like. Here are some of the challenges you may face:

- Your dog may not be willing to drop his toy in exchange for the treats in your hand. Try dropping the treats on the floor in a little Hansel and Gretel trail. Lots of dogs are more willing to give up their valued possession if the treats are within easy reach on the floor. Then, while he is following the trail to your hand that's still holding a reservoir of treats, pick up the KONG with your other hand.
- Your dog may lose interest in his toy after he realizes you have yummy treats in your hand. Try using less valuable treats, or a more valuable chew toy. Or simply play the game when he already happens to be chewing on one of his toys.
- Your dog may guard valuable resources. If he growls, snaps or even stiffens and looks angry when you try to trade with him, you should STOP practicing this exercise and seek the help of a qualified and positive training professional to help you resolve the resource guarding challenge. Meanwhile, supervise him very closely to prevent his access to forbidden objects so you don't put yourself at risk for being bitten because you have to take something away from him.

Note: I continue to trade my dogs for a treat when I want something they have throughout their entire lives—it keeps them happy and willing to give things up when I need them to.

Counter-conditioning to modify guarding

Here is one of my favorite protocols for modifying guarding behavior. (Note: If at any time you elicit a growl or other guarding behavior, you are too close and/or have proceeded too quickly):

1. Tether your dog to an eye bolt affixed to the wall for that purpose, or to a solid, heavy object. Give him a valuable chew object (not a KONG—it will roll out of his reach!), or a small bowl of food.

2. Have a good supply of toss-able high-value treats. (Chicken does not work well for this—it's too messy and hard to accurately toss). Small bits of cheese or meat work well.

3. Walk past your dog at a safe distance. Depending on the dog, this may be six to eight feet beyond the end of the tether, or it may be closer. As you pass him, toss several high-value treats near the bowl or chewy, where he can easily reach them. Keep walking—do not pause to toss. If your dog growls, lunges or shows other obvious guarding behavior you are too close.

Walk past at a safe distance from your tethered dog eating from his bowl, and toss treats to begin modifying resource guarding behavior.

4. Repeat Step 3 until, as you approach, you see your dog starting to look up in happy anticipation of the treats you are going to toss. When he does this consistently, decrease the distance by a few inches.

5. Continue passing by and dropping treats, gradually decreasing distance when he is consistently happy at each new distance.

Gradually decrease distance from your tethered dog eating from his bowl, and continue tossing treats.

6. When he is happy with you walking past at a distance close enough to touch him, pause as you pass and feed him a treat from your hand. Then walk on.

7. When he stays happy with your pause-and-feed, gradually increase the length of time you pause and feed. The increase should be no more than one to two seconds. As you increase the length of your pause, start talking to him in a happy voice as you feed.

8. When you can pause for ten seconds and he stays happy, occasionally bend slightly and drop a treat into his bowl or next to his chewy, then feed some more from your hand and walk on.

9. Repeat, gradually increasing the number of times you bend and drop.

10. Now gradually increase how much you bend over until you can touch the bowl or chewy. Remember, if you see any sign of tension you have moved too quickly. Back up a few steps and continue more slowly from there.

11. Finally, as you are pausing, bending and feeding, occasionally play the Trade game, always returning the bowl or object to him after he has happily allowed you to take it.

12. Now start the protocol over again at Step 1 with the next most reliable family member. Continue until your dog is comfortable with all family members approaching him, then repeat with trustworthy visitors, again starting with Step 1.

Walk Away protocol

The "Walk Away" protocol is another excellent and effective approach to modifying resource guarding. I was introduced to this protocol only recently by friend and fellow behavior professional, Kelly Fahey, PMCT2. Fahey created this approach to modifying resource guarding based on the innovative "Drop It" protocol developed by training and behavior professional Chirag Patel, BSc (Hons) CPDT-KA, DipCABT. (See Patel's "Drop It" protocol here: *www.youtube.com/watch?v=ndTiVOCNY4M.*) With Fahey's method, you begin by teaching your dog an operant behavior in response to the "Walk Away" cue, while at the same time giving him a positive classical association with that cue:

1. Say "Walk Away!" in a cheerful voice and toss several treats on the ground. Point at the treats as the dog finds them (at a safe distance if your dog is very guardy). Repeat eight to twelve times (or more) until dog eagerly responds to cue.

Begin the Walk Away procedure by pointing to treats as the dog finds them.

2. Place a neutral (not valuable to dog) object on the ground—a traffic cone, a statue, etc. When dog sniffs it, say "Walk Away!" and toss several treats on the ground two to four feet from the object. Point at the treats as the dog finds them (at a safe distance if your dog is very guardy).

Repeat at least eight to twelve times (or more) until your dog immediately moves away from the object in response to the cue. Use a variety of objects if necessary.

Practice "Walk Away" with a neutral object.

3. Place a low-value (to the dog) object on the ground—perhaps an insignificant toy. When dog sniffs it, say "Walk Away!" and toss several treats on the ground two to four feet from the object. Point at the treats as the dog finds them (at a safe distance if your dog is very guardy). Repeat at least eight to twelve times (or more) until your dog immediately moves away from the object in response to the cue. Use a variety of objects if necessary.

4. Place a medium-value (to the dog) object on the ground. When dog sniffs it, say "Walk Away!" and toss several treats on the ground two to four feet from the object. Point at the treats as the dog finds them (at a safe distance if your dog is very guardy). Repeat at least eight to twelve times (or more) until your dog immediately moves away from the object in response to the cue. Use a variety of objects if necessary.

5. Place a high-value (to the dog) object on the ground. When dog sniffs it, say "Walk Away!" and toss several treats on the ground two to four feet from the object. Point at the treats as the dog finds them (at a safe distance if your dog is very guardy). Repeat at least eight to twelve times (or more) until your dog immediately moves away from the object in response to the cue. Use a variety of objects if necessary.

6. Place an empty food bowl on the ground. When dog sniffs it, say "Walk Away!" and toss several treats on the ground two to four feet from the object. Point at the treats as the dog finds them (at a safe distance if your dog is very guardy). Repeat at least eight to twelve times (or more) until your dog immediately moves away from the bowl in response to the cue.

7. Put a handful of low-value food (dry kibble) in a food bowl and place it on the ground. When dog sniffs it, say "Walk Away!" and toss several treats on the ground two to four feet from the object. Point at the treats as the dog finds them (at a safe distance if your dog is very guardy). Repeat at least eight to twelve times (or more) until your dog immediately moves away from the bowl in response to the cue.

8. Put a handful of mid-value food (dry kibble mixed with a little canned) in a food bowl and place it on the ground. When dog sniffs it, say "Walk Away!" and toss several treats on the ground two to four feet from the object. Point at the treats as the dog finds them (at a safe distance if your dog is very guardy). Repeat at least eight to twelve times (or more) until your dog immediately moves away from the bowl in response to the cue.

9. Put a handful of high-value food (canned food or meat) in a food bowl and place it on the ground. When dog sniffs it, say "Walk Away!" and toss several treats on the ground two to four feet from the object. Point at the treats as the dog finds them (at a safe distance if your dog is very guardy). Repeat at least eight to twelve times (or more) until your dog immediately moves away from the bowl in response to the cue.

10. When dog is relaxed and happily moving away from objects and/or food bowls, add a "pick up the object or bowl" step into the protocol. Say "Walk Away!" and toss treats, then pick up the object/bowl, hand feed treats, and put object/bowl back on ground as you toss a few additional treats near the object/bowl.

Note: If at any point during the protocol you see tension or signs of aggression in your dog, back up one to three steps (or more!) and proceed again more slowly, with more repetitions at each step. And, as always, if you're not comfortable working with your dog's behavior yourself, seek the assistance of a qualified force-free behavior professional.

Most important, if you see guarding behavior in your dog, or you're considering adopting a shelter dog who may have some resource guarding behaviors, don't panic. Your dog isn't evil, he's just expressing his desire to maintain possession of something he finds valuable. In fact, recent studies indicate that resource guarding behavior identified in behavior assessments is less of a problem in adoptive homes than shelter workers have feared for decades. So relax, consider the behavior from your dog's perspective, empathize and start teaching him that you're not a threat to his good stuff.

CHAPTER 14

Resource Guarding: Dog-Dog

Dogs guard their resources, sometimes quite fiercely. This is most troublesome when they guard from humans, but can also get them in boiling hot water when they guard from other dogs. That said, some dog-dog guarding behavior is quite appropriate and acceptable. The wise dog owner not only knows the difference between appropriate and inappropriate guarding, she also knows when and how to intervene, manage and modify.

Resource guarding scenarios

If dogs didn't guard their resources from other dogs they'd be in danger of starving—in the wild and in multi-dog households. It's this survival instinct that triggers everything from the canine dirty look known as a "hard stare" to the ferocious, blood-letting, sometimes-fatal battles that can occur when dogs fight over valuable, mutually-coveted resources: food, toys, objects, locations, beds and human attention.

There are several different scenarios that can occur when one dog chooses to guard something from another, ranging from a very healthy, normal interaction to those that risk the very lives of one or more of the combatants. Here are five scenarios in increasing levels of intensity:

1. **Ideal—Dog A and Dog B are both appropriate:** The ideal resource guarding scenario probably plays itself out frequently in multi-dog households, dog parks, doggie daycares and any place dogs randomly gather. It looks something like this: Dog A is chewing happily on [insert any valuable resource here]. Dog B approaches, curious. Dog A gives Dog B "the look." Dog B quickly defers, saying, "Oh, excuse me!" by calmly turning and walking away. No harm done. Much of the time the dogs' owner isn't even aware that this occurred.

With his whale eye and snarl, this dog is sending the approaching dog a clear message that he doesn't want to share his space. As long as the other dog complies, this isn't necessarily a problem.

2. **Second Best—Dog B is inappropriate but Dog A defers:** Dog A is chewing on [insert resource]. Dog B approaches. Dog A gives Dog B "the look." Dog B gives Dog A "the look" back. Dog A defers, "Oops, sorry!" by dropping the resource and leaving. Dog B was inappropriate, but Dog A didn't want to argue about it. The danger here is that somewhere along the line Dog A may get fed up with Dog B's inappropriate behavior and decide not to defer.

3. **Now We're in Trouble, Part I—Dog A is inappropriate:** Dog A is chewing on [insert valuable resource]. Dog B approaches. Dog B would defer if warned, but rather than giving "the look," Dog A leaps into action and attacks without giving Dog B the opportunity to defer.

4. **Now We're in Trouble, Part II—Dog B is socially inept:** Dog A is chewing on [insert valuable resource]. Dog B approaches. Dog A gives "the look." Dog B is oblivious, and keeps blundering forward, until Dog A feels compelled to escalate the intensity of his message, to aggression if necessary, to get his point across.

5. **Now We're in Trouble, Part III—Dog B is inappropriate and Dog A doesn't defer:** Dog A is chewing on [insert valuable resource]. Dog B approaches. Dog A gives "the look." Dog B gives Dog A "the look" back. Instead of deferring, Dog A takes offense and escalates his aggressive behavior to maintain possession of his resource. Dog B reciprocates with increased aggression, and a serious fight ensues.

The same five scenarios can apply to other guarding situations: the dog who doesn't want to share his sticks or toys, who becomes tense if another dog approaches him on his bed, or who claims his owner's total and undivided attention all for himself. So whether it's food or some other valuable possession your dog is guarding, what do you do about it?

Beware: Be aware

First, you have to be aware of the guarding tension. It's hard to miss in Scenarios 3, 4 and 5, but if you have dogs engaged in one of the first two you may have overlooked it. Time to sit up and take notice! With Scenario 1, where both dogs respond appropriately, all you need to do is keep an eye on things and breathe a sigh of relief. As long as the pattern repeats itself, you needn't worry. You just need to stay calmly observant and take note if the pattern changes—if, for example, Dog B is slower to defer over time, which may cause an increase in Dog A's tension and possibly escalate to higher intensity guarding. Many dogs live happily together their entire lives politely signaling and deferring in relation to valuable resources. That's how it's supposed to work—perfectly appropriate and normal.

If you see subtle signs of increasing tension, however, or if you see Scenario 2 behavior, where Dog B is bullying Dog A into giving up the resource, you have potential trouble brewing. It's possible that Dog B will calmly defer for the rest of the dogs' lives together. You could continue to observe, and intervene only if things start to escalate. Maybe they never will. Or you could intervene with management and/or modification now, before you have significant relationship damage to repair, and a more difficult behavior modification challenge.

Of course, anything beyond Scenario 2 behavior requires immediate action in the form of management and, if you choose to do so, modification.

A first glance this looks like fun play between these two dogs. But while the older dog on the left appears somewhat low key about the play, a closer look suggests he's a little reluctant to fully engage because the younger dog on the right is very intense and, in fact, is not happy about sharing her toy.

Manage!

In case you haven't figured it out yet, I'm a huge fan of management. If your dog's list of guardable items is relatively short and the dog-dog guarding interactions are reasonably predictable, then management may be a realistic option. Only feed them their meals or give them pig ears when they are safely crated or closed in separate rooms. If you have a toy guarder, do toy-play with the dogs separately, and put coveted toys away when the dogs are together. Case closed.

If, however, battles are likely to erupt unexpectedly over an ever-growing list of miniscule triggers—a crumb dropped on the floor, a preferred resting spot on the rug, the hallway to the kitchen, equitably-delivered treats to both dogs, a rapidly-growing radius around a valued human—then modification is in order. Of course you'll manage in the meantime, but since management always carries a risk of failure and guarding battles can be fierce, the more generalized the guarding, the more critically important it becomes to convince your dogs to act appropriately with other dogs in the presence of high-value resources.

Modify

Remember that aggression is caused by cumulative stress that pushes a dog over his aggression threshold. We're all grumpier when we're stressed. Begin your modification program by minimizing as many other stressors as possible in your dogs' world. That includes creating structure and predictability in their lives, exploring and treating any possible medical conditions that may be causing pain or distress, and eliminating the use of any coercive or pain-causing training tools and methods (shock, choke and prong collars, physical or harsh verbal punishment). At the same time, incorporate calmness-inducing products and procedures such as increased aerobic exercise, the *Through a Dog's Ear* recordings (a set of CDs consisting of bio-acoustically engineered soothing classical piano music that has been shown to reduce dogs' heart rates available at *www.throughadogsear.com*), Thundershirts or Anxiety Wraps, calming massage and TTouch (a body work program that goes beyond simple massage: *www.ttouch.com/*).

There are a few different options for modifying resource guarding behavior between dogs. You can classically condition Dog A (the guarder) to love having another dog around him even in the presence of valuable resources; you can operantly condition Dog A to perform a different response when he's in possession of a valuable resource and another dog approaches; and you can operantly condition Dog B to avoid the guarder when he has a valuable resource. If you are not confident about your ability to safely implement these protocols, be sure to seek the assistance of a force-free behavior professional to help you get started. Here's how these each work:

Counter-Condition Dog A

The point of counter-conditioning is to change Dog A's emotional response to the proximity of Dog B in the presence of a guardable resource. This procedure will require dogs with very solid sit-stays and down-stays. Alternatively, you can use tethers. It's critically important that Dog A not be triggered to guard during these training sessions; awareness of threshold distance and the dogs' proximity to each other is paramount.

Step 1: Start with the two dogs sitting a few feet from each other—farther, if necessary to avoid guarding behavior. Have a bowl of pea-sized high-value treats. Give a treat to Dog B (the non-guarder), and then give one to Dog A, accompanied by happy-voice praise. If the dogs are so far apart you have to walk some distance to get to Dog A, start praising as you walk. Repeat until you see Dog A brighten noticeably when Dog B gets his treat—this tells you he's made the association between Dog B getting a treat and the next delicious treat coming to him. This is the conditioned emotional response you are looking for—the physical manifestation of the emotional change that happens because of the pairing between the presence of the other dog and the arrival of a high-value treat.

If you start with the dogs far apart, when you have established a consistent CER with Dog A, gradually move them closer together, continuing with the counter-conditioning and achieving CERs at each new distance until the dogs are happily taking treats a few feet apart. Depending on your dogs, this could take one session…or many.

Step 2: Have a bowl of high-value treats. Hang out with Dog A in a good-sized quiet room with the door closed—watch TV, read a book, work on the computer…but don't feed him any treats. In fact, ignore him completely. After 20 to 30 minutes, bring Dog B into the room on leash and have him sit and stay a safe distance from Dog A (or tether him if his stay isn't rock solid). Feed Dog B a treat, then spend 20 to 30 seconds giving generous treats and praise to Dog A. Then remove Dog B from the room.

At varying intervals, bring Dog B back into the room and repeat the procedure—always bringing Dog B into the room before you make any move to reach for the treats in the bowl. Repeat until Dog A looks consistently happy—the CER—as you move to bring in Dog B.

Step 3: Repeat Step 2, but this time Dog A is in possession of a guardable resource—a bone, a toy, a favorite bed. If there are things he guards less intensely than others, start with a lower-value resource.

Tether Dog A with his resource as far from the door as possible, and do another 20- to 30-minute hang-out before bringing in Dog B. Step in the door with Dog B, have him sit and stay (or tether), feed him a treat, and then do your 20- to 30-second praise-and-treat routine with Dog A. Repeat until you have a consistent CER—Dog A brightens happily when you enter the room with Dog B. As you do these repetitions, occasionally encourage brief eye contact between the dogs several times at each distance, so that trigger gets built into the procedure. If eye contact triggers significantly greater intensity from Dog A, stay at the door until that intensity goes away and you are getting consistent CERs, even with eye contact.

Gradually move closer with Dog B, obtaining consistent CERs at each new distance before moving closer again. Remember to do some eye contact. When you have closed the distance by half, mark that spot and start over again at the full distance, but this time with Dog A untethered. This should not trigger any tension from Dog A, and you should be able to move closer to him with Dog B, still being careful to watch for any signs of uneasiness. *Be careful! If you think you are going too slowly, slow down.* It's easy to fall into the trap of thinking you're not accomplishing anything if you don't see tension, but in fact the exact opposite is true. You want to proceed so carefully and slowly that you *don't* ever see tension!

Step 4: Repeat Step 3 with the same value resource, in all the rooms in the house, until you have consistent CERs everywhere. If you have multiple dogs that Dog A guards from, repeat Steps 1 through 3 with each of the dogs. Then repeat in gradually larger groups (two dogs, three dogs, etc.) until Dog A offers consistent CERs regardless of what dog, how may dogs or what room.

Step 5: Go back to Step 3, again with Dog A tethered, but now in possession of a somewhat more valuable resource. Repeat all steps with all dogs, individually at first, then in larger groups, until Dog A offers consistent CERs regardless of what dog or what room. Continue up the resource-value ladder until Dog A shows no sign of tension.

Step 6: Do occasional "cold trials" without the set-up and repetition—a deliberate "management failure"—counter-conditioning meets real life. Do at least one cold trial per day, and if you see tension reappearing, go back and do repetitions of the procedure at whatever step is necessary for your dog to regain his equilibrium. Then move through the steps to completion; this will probably progress much more quickly than the first time through.

Operant conditioning for Dog A

Resource guarding behavior lends itself beautifully to the Constructional Aggression Treatment operant conditioning protocol developed by Dr. Jesus Rosales Ruiz and Kellie Snider, MA. (See Chapter 8.) Our Dog A gets tense and eventually aggressive because he is concerned that the approaching dog is a threat to his valuable resource. These aggressive distance-increasing signals are often successful in making the other dog go away, hence they are reinforced, and behaviors that are reinforced are repeated.

To use the CAT procedure, tether Dog A with a low- to moderate-value guardable resource, and approach from a distance with Dog B. If you know Dog A begins showing signs of guarding at a distance of 15 feet, start at 25 feet. As you approach, watch Dog A for any small sign of tension. The instant you see it, stop with Dog B, mark the spot, and wait. As soon as you see any decrease in Dog A's tension, any sign of relaxation, quickly turn and walk away with Dog B, back to the 25-foot distance.

Pause there for at least 15 seconds (longer if you think Dog A needs more recovery time), and then repeat, returning to the marker at the spot where you stopped before. Continue these repetitions until you see no sign of tension from Dog A when you arrive at the marker with Dog B. On your next approach move two to six inches closer or less (six inches may be too much of an advance at one time for some dogs, especially once you are very near to Dog A, so don't be discouraged if you need to stop at a shorter distance), and mark that spot. You will likely see tension again at this distance. Repeat approaches and departures as described above at this distance until the tension is gone, then decrease distance slightly again.

What you are doing with this procedure is teaching Dog A that a new behavior—acting calm and relaxed—makes the threat to his resource go away. As he continues to deliberately act calm and relaxed he actually becomes calm and relaxed, and eventually no longer feels threatened by the approach of Dog B. Ideally you will see crossover, where he acts very friendly and affiliative as Dog B approaches, offering distance-decreasing signals instead of his previous repertoire of distance-increasing signals. When you've worked through the procedure with low- to moderate-value resources, repeat with high-value resources.

With counter-conditioning, you change your dog's emotional response, and as a result his behavior changes. With operant conditioning (CAT), you change your dog's behavioral response, and as a result his emotional response changes.

Operant conditioning for Dog B

You can also operantly teach Dog B a new behavior in the presence of Dog A and a valuable resource. This is a useful second line of defense, in combination with modifying the behavior of the guarder. You can teach Dog B to withdraw on your cue, and if Dog A gives noticeable warning, such as a hard stare or a lip curl, you can also teach Dog B to withdraw in response to those cues. The advantage of a cue from Dog A is that it happens, and Dog B responds by leaving, even if you're not there to give your cue. Eventually you may find that the mere presence of "Dog A with resource" becomes the cue for Dog B to leave, which is just fine and dandy. If you see Dog B leaving the room before the cue, go ahead and reinforce that—it's a good thing!

When the cue is given (yours or Dog A's), guide (lure or prompt) Dog B to a specified target, ideally in another room. Throw a treat-and-praise fest there for Dog B, and hang out with him there for several minutes before returning to Dog A's room and repeating the process. Dog B should soon be dashing to the other room when the cue is given—either yours or Dog A's lip curl.

So what happens if Dog A is in the designated target room with a valuable resource? Great question! It's a good idea to operantly condition Dog B to a second target location in a different room. When Dog A is in Room X, Dog B learns to target to the spot in Room Y. But if Dog A is in Room Y, Dog B learns to target to a spot in Room X. The more target spots there are available to Dog B, the more quickly he can get to his safe zones.

Teach Dog A to Walk Away

You can also use the Walk Away protocol presented in the previous chapter to modify and manage your dog's resource guarding behavior toward other dogs. Start by teaching Dog A the basic Walk Away protocol. When he can perform it easily, even with high-value resources, introduce Dog B at a below-threshold distance.

Have a second person bring Dog B into the room and stay far enough away that Dog A remains calm and relaxed. You may need to do this outside at first if Dog A's threshold is too great for indoor distances. Practice your Walk Away with Dog A, very gradually bringing Dog B closer. If you reach a point where Dog A is having difficulty with the Walk Away, you have come a little too close. Back up with Dog B, and keep practicing.

Depending on the intensity of Dog A's dog-dog guarding behavior, it may take many sessions for this to work, or you may see success in just a few sessions. The ultimate goal is that when you see potential trouble brewing, you can cheerfully ask Dog A to walk away and he will happily leave his resource, defusing the situation and allowing you to intervene without difficulty.

Use a mix of management and modification methods

Keep in mind that you are likely to always need some degree of management, even with your successful modification programs. For example, even if you've done a great job of modifying the behavior of a dog who tends to guard toys, the high arousal of a dog-to-dog game of tug carries a high likelihood of retriggering guarding aggression. Reserve his tug playing for games with you, and let him play romping and running games with his canine pals. Be smart. Manage as needed, keep your eyes open for signs of returning tension, and be prepared to do a little remedial modification as needed.

So there you have it. Select the method(s) that appeal to you and get started. It will do your heart good to see the lessening tension between your canine family members, and your guarder gains new associations and learns new behaviors without fear of losing his valuables to his four-legged siblings.

You might be wise to refer to your dog who "was" a resource guarder as a "recovering resource guarder," rather than consider him "fixed" or "cured." You may go for years without resource guarding issues. Still, don't let yourself be lured into a false sense of security. Always be aware of body language signals and possible tension between your dogs, and be aware that something could make him fall off the wagon.

CHAPTER 15

Aggression in a Multi-Dog Household

Knowledgeable dog people are quite aware that not all dogs get along with each other, despite the fact that *canis lupus familiaris* (the domestic dog) is a social species. Hey, we humans are a social species, and we certainly don't all get along! Dog-dog aggression is unhappily common in our world. As a professional behavior consultant who works with aggression cases, I probably see more than my fair share of it. By far the most difficult and most distressing presentations of dog-dog aggression are cases of dogs in the same family who aren't getting along with each other.

The results of intra-pack aggression—a potentially dangerous and challenging behavior that can significantly diminish the quality of life for all members of the family, not just the canines.

I've had a spate of these clients recently. Even my own Lucy and Missy, a Cardigan Corgi and Australian Shepherd who don't always get along seamlessly, seem to have experienced an increase in relationship tensions this winter. I can't give you a tidy explanation as to why, but I'm beginning to put more stock in the explanation jokingly offered by a colleague who called it "snow aggression."

Stress happens

We do know that aggression is caused by stress. With the very rare exception of idiopathic aggression, aggression is the result of a stress load that pushes a dog over his bite threshold. You can compare it to incidents of "road rage" in humans. When you read about the man who pulls out his .38 revolver because someone cut him off on the freeway and blows away the unfortunate offending driver, you can bet there was more going on for him than just a simple traffic violation. This is the guy who was likely laid off his job, lost his retirement investments to Bernie Madoff, had his wife tell him this morning that she was leaving him, and just got notice in the mail that the bank is foreclosing on his McMansion. Getting cut off on the freeway is simply the last straw—the final stressor that pushes him over his "bite threshold."

So it is for dogs. When tensions increase between Missy and Lucy, I need to look for possible added stressors in their environment that are pushing them closer to—and yes, sometimes over—their bite threshold. From that perspective, "snow aggression" is a real possibility: with recent record snowfalls reaching a total of 50 inches here, the resulting decrease in exercise opportunities as well as higher stress levels of human family members who aren't fond of snow (guilty!) can certainly be stressors for the canine family members.

Triggers

To resolve aggression issues between your own dogs, you'll want to identify not just the immediate trigger for the aggression—fighting over a pig ear, for example—but also everything in your dogs' lives that may be stressful to them. The more stressors you can remove from their world, the further away they are from using their teeth on each other—the canine equivalent of a duel with pistols.

It's often relatively easy to identify the immediate trigger for your dogs' mutual aggression. It's usually whatever happened just before the appearance of the hard stare, posturing, growls and sometimes the actual fight.

Tension over resources is a common trigger. Dog A is lying on his bed, happily chewing his deer antler, when Dog B approaches. Dog A tenses, signaling to Dog B, "This is mine and I'm not sharing." In the best of worlds, Dog B defers by looking away, saying in canine speak, "Oh, no worries, I was just passing through." When things go wrong, however, a fight breaks out. Dog B's approach was the trigger, sometimes even if he had no interest in the chew item—if Dog A launched into full combat without proper warning, or if Dog B failed to notice or failed to heed the warning.

Remember that resources aren't just food and high-value chews; a guardable resource can be a high-value human, a coveted bed, a spot on the sofa or access to a doorway. The stressor in these cases is fairly obvious—the dog's anxiety over the possibility of losing or having to share his treasured possession.

Some other triggers may be less obvious. If a dog is in pain, but not showing it, the mere proximity of a packmate who has inadvertently bumped her in the past could be a trigger. Dogs can be notoriously stoic about pain, especially slowly developing arthritis or bilateral pain; if both hips hurt, it doesn't do any good to limp! The undiagnosed arthritic dog may become defensively aggressive in anticipation of being hurt by a livelier canine pal as she tries to forestall painful contact. The resulting behavior looks to the owner like "unprovoked" aggression.

When you have identified your dogs' triggers, you can manage the environment to reduce trigger incidents and minimize outright conflict. This is critically important to a successful modification program. Dogs who are hearing or sight impaired, or those losing those faculties due to aging, and those not fluent in dog body language (young puppies, or dogs not well-socialized with other dogs) may not be very good at perceiving and/or understanding subtle or even blatant signals from Dog A. Management becomes even more important for these dogs' safety. The more often the dogs fight, the more tension there is between them; the more practiced they become at the undesirable behaviors, the better they get at fighting and the harder it will be to make it go away. To say nothing of the increased likelihood that sooner or later someone—dog or human—will be badly injured.

Stressors

Stressors, on the other hand, can happen anytime and be anywhere—or everywhere. Remember that it's the sum total of a dog's stressors that push him over his bite threshold, so the more of these you can identify and get rid of, the more you'll ease tensions between your canine family members. When I sit down with a client for an aggression consult we create a complete list of all the stressors we can think of for the dog or dogs in question. Then we discuss possible strategies for making stressors go away, and assign one or more strategies to each of the listed stressors.

Next, I help the client create action plans for two or three of the stressors on the list to address first (management plans go into place immediately for all stressors), starting with the one the client is most concerned about—in this case, the dog-dog aggression.

Trouble brewing here—the Corgi on the right is stiff and tense, ahead of the vertical, bullying the Border Collie every time she moves. The Border Collie is being very appeasing—making herself small, leaning away and not making direct eye contact. This could be a significant stressor and a major problem if the dogs lived in the same household. Fortunately they do not.

Which strategies should be used with which stressors?

There are five major strategies that can be used to modify a dog's reaction to the various stressors that might trigger aggression. There are many other possibilities. The strategies are listed A to E below. Following that is a list of common stressors with an indicator of which strategies are most appropriate for each one. My clients' lists usually number between ten and 20 identified stressors. Be sure to include even those things that may cause mild stress—the more stressors you can remove, the better.

Strategies

A. Change dog's opinion of the stressor through the use of counter-conditioning and desensitization.

B. Teach the dog a new behavioral response using operant conditioning.

C. Manage the dog's environment to minimize exposure to the stressor.

D. Get rid of the stressor.

E. Live with it (most appropriate for low-level stressors).

Stressors with strategies designated

1. The other dog (A)
2. People passing by outside the living room window (A/C, block access to window)
3. Threats to his resources (A/B/C)

4. Doorbell ringing (A/B)

5. Car rides (A/E)

6. Trips to the vet hospital (A/E)

7. Nail trimming (A, counter-conditioning as described in Chapter 11/B, teach him to scrape his nails on an abrasive surface)

8. Thunder (A/C, possible use of appropriate anti-anxiety medication)

9. Fireworks (A/C, possible use of appropriate anti-anxiety medication/E)

10. Arthritis (C, consider use of pain-reducing medication)

11. Recurring ear infections (D, explore medical treatment and diet—a recurring ear infection may result from dietary sensitivities)

12. Underground shock fence (D)

13. Prong collar (D)

14. Use of physical and harsh verbal corrections (punishment) (D)

15. Owner stress (C/D)

Aggression modification (Strategy A)

My first choice with most clients is Strategy A—changing the dogs' opinions of each other through counter-conditioning and desensitization. This involves the use of controlled set-ups—with both dogs on leash at threshold distance (that distance at which they see each other, are alert and a little concerned, but not highly aroused). If one dog's threshold distance is less than the other's and the second dog shows no concern at all, start your program at the greater distance—you will eventually decrease the distance to the point the second dog is concerned as well.

Counter-conditioning and desensitization for modifying intra-pack aggression involves changing your dogs' association with each other from negative to positive. The easiest way to give most dogs a positive association is with very high-value, really yummy treats. As I've said before, I like to use chicken—canned, baked or boiled, since most dogs love chicken and it's a low-fat, low-calorie food.

Here's how the process works:

1. Determine the distance at which your dogs can be in each other's presence and be alert or wary but not extremely fearful or aroused. This is called the threshold distance. If one dog has a greater threshold distance than the other (often the case), work at the greater distance.

2. With you holding Dog A on leash, have your helper appear with Dog B at threshold distance X. The instant your dog sees the other, start feeding bits of chicken, non-stop. Your helper will feed chicken to her dog, too, the instant he notices your dog.

3. After several seconds, have the helper step out of sight with Dog B, and you both stop feeding chicken.

4. Keep repeating Steps 1 through 3 until the sight of the other dog at distance X consistently causes both dogs to look at their handlers with a happy smile and a "Yay! Where's my chicken?" expression. This is the physical presentation of the dogs' conditioned emotional response (CER); each dog's association with the other at threshold distance X is now positive, so they can deliberately look at you to get their chicken, rather than staying intensely focused on each other.

5. Now you need to increase the intensity of the stimulus by increasing the length of time Dog B stays in sight. Continue to feed chicken when they are in view of each other, occasionally pausing to let them look again, and immediately feeding chicken when they do.

6. When length of time seems to make no difference to either dog—you're getting a consistent "Yay, where's my chicken?" response regardless of how long Dog B stays in view, increase intensity again, this time by increasing Dog B's movement. Have the handler walk back and forth with her dog, still at distance X, slowly at first, then with more energy, even adding in some other behaviors such as sit, down and roll over.

7. Now you're ready to start decreasing distance by moving Dog A a little closer to the location where Dog B will appear. When you obtain consistent CERs from both dogs at each new distance you can decrease the distance a little more, until both dogs are happy to be very near each other.

8. Then return to your original threshold distance and increase the intensity of the stimulus by having Dog B move around more and more, as you gradually decrease distance and obtain CERs from both dogs along the way, until they are delighted to be near each other.

9. Now go back to your starting distance and increase intensity again, by having both dogs move more naturally as the distance decreases, offering CERs at each new distance before you come any closer, until they can be within six feet of each other, moving around, still relaxed and happy about chicken.

10. Finally, find ways for your dogs to engage separately in mutually enjoyable activities together. If they both enjoy car rides, take them for a drive, but be sure they are seat-belted or crated far enough apart to avoid any tension. If they love hiking, take them on "parallel" walks, one with you, one with your training partner, with humans between them at first, and eventually with dogs between humans when you're sure their emotions are appropriate. Parallel swims, for dogs who love the water (far enough apart to be safe!), can work well too.

You can also tether the dogs in the evening, when the house tends to be quieter and more relaxed as family members settle in to watch their favorite television shows. Tether the dogs far enough apart, giving each something delicious like a bully stick or marrow bone to keep them happy. Let the dogs enjoy their yummy treats, in the same room, at a safe distance from each other.

When you feel the dogs are ready to finally interact with each other again, be careful not to undo all your hard work. You might first let them greet through a barrier, such as a baby gate or exercise pen. It's useful to condition both dogs to a muzzle over the period you're desensitizing them to each other (in separate sessions), so the first time you're ready for them to actually interact you're confident they can't hurt each other.

The more intense the relationship between the two dogs, the more challenging their behavior is to modify. The more negative interactions they've had, the more injuries they've sustained, the longer the tension has been going on, and the stronger their emotions, the longer it will take to reprogram their response to each other. If they were good friends at one time, it's likely to be easier than if they've always been aggressive with each other. Always remember to seek the help of a qualified force-free behavior professional if you don't feel competent and confident about working with your dogs on your own.

Teach a new operant behavior (Strategy B)

A second option is Strategy B—teaching a new operant behavior in response to each other using the CAT procedure. While one of the challenges of a CAT procedure for dog-dog aggression is getting the dog to generalize to lots of different dogs, when we're working with intra-pack aggression, the two dogs in question only need to learn to like each other, so the generalization piece isn't necessary. Still another Strategy B operant approach is the BAT procedure. Again, since the dogs only need to learn to like each other, the generalization piece of the BAT operant learning protocol is not a barrier to success.

If one or both of the dogs are ready to do battle on sight, they must be strictly managed and kept separate from each other except when you're doing your controlled modification procedure with them. If the aggression is more predictable and situational, the dogs can be together as long as you can manage and prevent the trigger(s) from causing conflict.

More tips for lowering environmental stress

There are a host of other things you can do to lower general stress in the environment. Of course, a complete medical workup, including a full thyroid panel, is mandatory for any significant behavior problem, and especially for aggression. Any medical condition that causes either of your dogs to feel out of sorts is a massive stress-contributor. Trying to modify aggression while one of your dogs suffers from an untreated medical condition is akin to pushing a behavioral boulder uphill. You must rule out or identify and treat any medical contributors to your dogs' behavior in order to receive full benefit from your modification efforts.

Exercise can be immensely helpful in minimizing overall tension. Not only does physical activity use up excess energy that might otherwise feed your dogs' aggressive behaviors (a tired dog is a well-behaved dog), but also during exercise your dog's body releases various chemicals that generate a feeling of well-being, including endorphins and norepinephrine: an exercised dog is a happy dog! Happy dogs are simply less likely to fight.

Even the food you feed your dog can have an impact on his behavior. Poor quality protein can interfere with a dog's ability to make use of the serotonin that occurs naturally in his system. There is also scientific evidence that corn consumption is associated with a marked reduction in brain serotonin. Serotonin is a neurotransmitter that helps regulate mood and sleep, and also affects memory and learning. Corn-free foods that utilize high-quality, human-grade protein contribute to your dogs' behavioral health as well as their physical health.

Basic training enables you and your dog to communicate more easily with each other (which is less stressful for both of you), and helps your dog understand how his world works—which makes his world less stressful for him. A good training program emphasizes structure and consistency, both of which make a dog's world more predictable. Predictability equals less stress; an unpredictable life is stressful.

If you've ever had a massage, you know how calming touch can be. Dogs aren't that different from us; you can calm and soothe your dog with physical touch through canine massage. If you combine your calming touch sessions with aromatherapy—burn a lavender candle while you massage—you can utilize your dog's "ahhhhhhhhhhhhhhh" association with the lavender scent to help him be calm in more stressful environments by spritzing the scent on a scarf that you tie around his neck, or on the bedding of his crate. *Note: All behavior-enhancing substances have the potential to have a* ***paradoxical effect****—doing the exact opposite of what we want. If you see this happening, stop using the product. If you are using prescription medications, talk to your veterinarian about how to wean your dog off the medication gradually, rather than going cold turkey.*

Other environmental stress reducers can include products such as Adaptil (also known as Comfort Zone, Dog Appeasing Pheromone, or DAP), a synthetic substance that mimics the pheromones emitted by a mother dog when she's nursing puppies, intended to keep the puppies calm; *Through a Dog's Ear* CDs; the ThunderShirt, or even a snug T-shirt, which can have some of the same effects.

When your best efforts fail

Dog-dog aggression in your home can feel overwhelming. It can, in fact, be dangerous, if fights erupt regularly and you try to intervene. Many an owner has been bitten trying to break up fights between her own dogs. The stress that the constant tension generates can damage the quality of your own life, as well as your dogs'.

When a situation feels beyond your ability to cope, your first best option is to find a qualified force-free behavior consultant in your area who can help you implement appropriate management and modification procedures, to keep everyone safe and to start making change happen in your dogs' mutual relationships. A consult with a veterinarian who is well-educated in behavior, or even a veterinary behaviorist, should also be on your list, not only for that all-important medical workup, but also for the consideration of psychotropic behavior modification drugs, if and when appropriate, to help your dog's brain be more receptive to your modification efforts.

If you feel you've done your best and peace isn't in the cards for your pack, it's okay to admit that some dogs will never get along, and you have had the misfortune to adopt two who don't. If that's the case, your options are:

- A lifetime of scrupulous management
- Rehoming one of the dogs
- Euthanasia

Some trainers say "Management always fails." In truth, management does have a high risk of failure, perhaps with potentially dire consequences. The risk is even higher if there are children in the home—not only because they're more likely to forget to close doors and latch gates, but also because they are at greater risk of injury themselves if they are in the vicinity when a fight happens. Still, I know of several dog owners who have successfully implemented lifetime management protocols for dogs who didn't get along, and felt that their own quality of life, as well as that of their dogs, was above reproach.

Rehoming (see Chapter 19) can be a reasonable option, especially if the dog being considered for placement has no other significant inappropriate behaviors, and if he can be rehomed to an "only dog" home, or one with dogs he's known to get along well with. Of course, it can be challenging to find an experienced, appropriate home for a dog with a known aggression behavior problem, but it may be possible, particularly if he's wonderful aside from the relationship issue.

No one wants to think of euthanizing an otherwise healthy member of their canine family. Still, if you've done all you can reasonably do given the limits of your abilities and resources, and you've not been able to create a safe environment for your family and one of the dogs can't be rehomed, then euthanasia is not an inappropriate decision. It will be a terribly painful decision for you to make, and you'll always feel guilt and regret about not finding the solution to the problem, although perhaps not as much guilt and regret as you would if one of your dogs badly injured or killed the other, or worse, a person.

Breaking up a dog fight

A dog fight that goes beyond a brief scuffle and doesn't resolve quickly is frightening to behold. In fact, it's one of the behavior scenarios most likely to result in significant injury to humans, not to mention the dogs. The first, most important thing to remember is keep yourself safe. After that, here are six things to do to try to end the conflict as quickly as possible, with minimal bloodshed. *(Note that even taking these precautions still doesn't guarantee you won't be bitten.):*

1. **Spray me a river:** Blast the dogs with water from a nearby hose—assuming a nearby hose with a powerful enough spray. An easily portable aversive such as lemon juice in a spray bottle can be an effective hose alternative. In a pinch, even a fire extinguisher makes a handy and effective fight-stopping tool. Citronella in a pressurized can (Spray Shield) may also work to break up a lower intensity scuffle—it doesn't hurt to have some on hand and easily accessible.

2. **Sound strategies:** Depending on the intensity of the fight, a loud yell might put it to rest. Try dropping one (or several) metal pans on the floor. A lit match held under a smoke detector alarm might also do the trick. Available at boating supply stores, a marine air horn can be effective at breaking up a fight. Warning: they are loud!

3. **An object lesson:** Keep your hands out of the danger zone by using a physical object to break up a fight. (You have to plan in advance.) Attach two handles to a sheet of plywood. When a fight happens, lower the board between the sparring dogs. The board will push them apart and provide a physical barrier between them to prevent a new grab. Dogfighters—and some Pit Bull owners who don't allow their dogs to fight but know the breed's potential—always carry a "parting stick" or "breaking stick" with them. (Note: I am *not* in *any way* endorsing dogfighting or dogfighters!!!!) This is often a carved hammer handle, tapered to a rounded point at one end. When dogs are locked in combat, the parting stick is forced between a dog's teeth and turned sideways to pry open the jaws. Caution: Parting sticks can break teeth, and a dog whose jaws have just been "parted" may turn on the person doing the parting. You can also use blankets to try to interrupt a fight. Tossed over fighters, one over each, blankets muffle outside stimuli, reducing arousal. This also allows humans to physically

separate the combatants by picking up the pups-in-a-blanket and pulling them apart with less risk of a serious bite; the blanket will cushion the effect of teeth on skin if the dog does whirl and bite.

4. **Air supply:** When life and limb are at stake, extreme measures may be called for. Wrap a leash round the aggressor's neck or twist the collar to cut off the dog's airflow. When he lets go for a breath of air, pull the dogs apart. You can also cover the dog's nose with a plastic bag to cut off the air supply. These are more challenging than they sound: it's difficult to get a leash around the neck of a dog who is "attached" by mouth to another dog; grabbing a collar to twist puts hands in close proximity to teeth; and the nose of a dog mid-fight is a moving target.

5. **Let's get physical:** I heard about (never tried) a rather drastic technique observed at a dog show decades ago. The elderly judge was a tiny woman. When two dogs got combative in her ring she had the handlers both grab their dogs and hold on tight. Then she took the dog on top by the tail and jammed her thumb up his rectum. He let go in an instant and whirled around to see what was happening. The judge excused the two dogs, calmly washed her hands and continued her classes. Note: A client of mine tried this recently. It didn't work for her.

6. **Smaller dogs:** Here's another approach for smallish dogs in a one-on-one fight. (It is not recommended for a multi-dog brawl.) Lift the rear of the clearly identified aggressor so he's suspended with forefeet barely touching the ground. The dog lets go, and the target can scoot free. Supposedly, in this position the dog is not able to turn on the human suspending him, although I'm not giving any guarantees.

None of these are force-free techniques, and they are methods I would only use in an emergency, not as regular training procedures. There are, of course, no guarantees for any of these methods—the best answer is management and modification. If you have dogs who fight, keep them apart, unless and until they learn to get along. The best of management plans can fail, however. If and when that fight happens, take a deep breath, resist your instincts to leap in the middle of the fray, quickly review your available options, and choose the one—or ones—that are most likely to work in that place and time. When the fight is over and no one is being rushed to the hospital in an ambulance, remember to take a moment to relax and breathe, and then congratulate yourself for your quick thinking.

CHAPTER 16

Reactive Rovers

Does your dog go ballistic when he sees another dog? If it's any consolation, you're not alone. What I call Reactive Rovers, dogs who become over-aroused in the presence of other dogs, make up at least half of my private consultation work.

Animal behavior professionals have ongoing discussions about why we seem to be seeing so many more Reactive Rovers than we did in the past. They have several theories, all probably containing some truth. Here are four of them:

1. Herding breeds like Border Collies and Australian Shepherds who enjoy great popularity in today's dog world are genetically programmed to be sensitive to direct eye contact and prone to having space issues. These dogs are likely to react to dogs who invade their space. Many breeds, Pit Bull Terriers and others, are also genetically programmed to respond with arousal to the presence of other dogs. The closer they are genetically to their dog fighting roots, the more likely they will be dog-reactive.

2. Whereas in times past dogs were given a great deal of freedom to roam in a community and learn how to play well with others, today's responsible dog owners keep their dogs safely confined at home. Dogs have less opportunity to learn how to act appropriately around other dogs and less chance to fulfill their need to socialize with members of their own species.

3. Once upon a time, dogs who misbehaved were simply left at home, or worse, euthanized. Today's dog owner is more likely to look for reasons—and solutions—for inappropriate canine behaviors and be more willing to invest resources to fix them. (This is a good thing!)

4. In recent years, high-arousal dog sports have taken center stage. Where competition obedience dogs are expected to be calm and controlled, albeit enthusiastic, today's Agility and Flyball dogs, for example, are encouraged to compete in a state of high excitement and arousal.

The term "dog-reactivity" covers a wide variety of behaviors, including:

- Fear reactive dogs who want to hide behind their humans' legs or run full speed away to escape the danger.
- Barrier/restraint-reactive dogs who get frustrated and aroused when they aren't allowed to greet every passing canine.
- Territorial dogs who react with strong aggressive challenges to any dogs who intrude on their perceived territories.
- Dogs who can't tolerate other dogs invading their close personal space.
- Those who simply feel a compelling need to read the riot act to every dog they see. Some dogs are selective, choosing a specific breed, color or sex, others are equal-opportunity reactors.

While not all reactive behavior manifests as aggression, much of it does to a lesser or greater degree. Some dogs react out of frustration. These are the dogs who are reactive when they are on leash and who seem to do just fine with other dogs when they are off leash. They are less likely to be truly aggressive, although with enough arousal they may become aggressive as well. Some owners are in denial about the aggressive element of their reactive dog's behavior. This is unfortunate, perhaps motivated by society's—and the insurance industry's—increasing aversion to unruly, potentially dangerous dogs. In the long run, however, it's more useful to acknowledge the behavior than ignore it.

Dog-reactive dogs are a threat to other dogs. They can put humans at risk of being bitten while breaking up dog fights or as victims of redirected aggression, and ultimately the dogs may lose their own lives if they injure another dog or person. At best, their quality of life diminishes as owners become less willing to overlook the behavior and more likely to leave their dog at home rather than risk an altercation or have to deal with the misbehavior in public.

The fact that many owners are willing to make the effort to modify dog-reactivity is encouraging, especially for the dogs. While a recovering reactive dog may never be a good candidate for dog park play, many can learn to control themselves in the presence of other canines, at least well enough to lead reasonably normal lives. Some even develop a close circle of friends with whom they can play without fear of eruption.

Staying below threshold

The most effective behavior modification programs create an environment where your dog can be around other dogs without over-reacting—where he can stay sub-threshold. That means presenting the trigger stimulus, in this case another dog or dogs, at an intensity below the one that causes your reactive dog to erupt into full arousal.

At this sub-threshold level, you can work to change the dog's opinion, association and resulting response to the presence of another dog through counter-conditioning. Here's how:

Begin by determining your dog's threshold distance—that distance where he'll notice another dog, become concerned but not go bonkers. Introduce a neutral dog on leash at this distance.

The instant your dog notices the other dog, start feeding him a very high-value treat, such as canned or boiled chicken. As long as he can see the other dog, keep feeding small bits of chicken. As soon as the other dog leaves, stop the chicken. Keep doing this until you notice a change in your dog's reaction. When the other dog enters the room, instead of tensing up and saying "Uh-oh, another dog," he turns to you with a doggie grin and says, "Yay! Where's my chicken?! (See Counter-conditioning and Desensitization in Chapter 8.) This is another example of obtaining a CER using counter-conditioning.

When you are getting a consistent CER from your dog every time the other dog enters, you can increase the intensity. You have several options. Choose one at a time, work for the CER at that intensity, then increase it again. If you increase intensity and your dog starts erupting at the presentation of the other dog, you've increased intensity too much or too soon. You may need to increase your initial threshold distance. Remember, you're trying to stay sub-threshold.

- **Distance:** Perhaps your initial threshold distance is 40 feet. When you get the CER reliably and consistently at 40 feet, you might decrease the distance to 39 feet. Or 35 feet. Or 30 feet. Some dogs can increase intensity in large leaps; most need smaller steps. You're generally better off to err on the side of caution, using smaller increments. **"Greedy trainer syndrome"** (trying to do too much too quickly) can get you in trouble!
- **Motion:** If your neutral dog was entering at 40 feet and stopping, have the dog walk back and forth at 40 feet, until you get a consistent CER. Then have the dog trot back and forth at 40 feet. You can vary the concept of motion—have the neutral dog stay still and instead walk with your dog. Do parallel walking with both dogs in motion, walking the same direction, with appropriate distance between them.
- **Number of dogs:** When you have a reliable and consistent CER with one neutral dog, add a second neutral dog. Then a third.
- **Size of dogs:** If your dog is more reactive to large dogs, you might start with a neutral dog in the 40- to 50-pound range, then move up to 50-60 pounds, 60-70 pounds, etc. Be sure to achieve a consistent CER each time before moving up to the next weight class.

- **Sounds:** Some dogs are reactive to the jingling tags of other dogs or the sound of another dog barking. Add jingly tags to your neutral dog, or use one or more neutral dogs who will bark on cue.
- **Angle of approach:** Many dogs feel greatly threatened by the direct approach of another dog—as they might encounter routinely when walking on a city sidewalk. Start with the neutral dog walking at a 90-degree angle to your reactive dog and gradually decrease the angle of approach until the neutral dog is walking directly toward you—but several feet off to the side so the dogs don't actually meet head on. This is a difficult exercise for a reactive dog—be sure you're getting consistent CERs each step of the way! *(Note: In the dog world, dogs don't often greet head on. Dogs tend to greet with more of an arc approach when checking out a new friend. Walking head on to an approaching dog isn't natural and causes a reactive dog to, well, react.)*

Work below threshold. This reactive dog is alert, focused on the aversive stimulus, but not barking and lunging.

Carefully control the intensity of stimulus for successful counter-conditioning. For this dog-reactive dog, the neutral dog is a good distance away and appears for a very short time before retreating behind the bushes.

Increase intensity by increasing the number of dogs.

Increase intensity by moving closer to multiple dogs.

Another increased intensity of stimulus: moving closer, making a more direct approach.

Head-on approach—most difficult for many reactive dogs.

As nice as set-ups are, unless you're a hermit, you and your dog will inevitably have real-life super threshold encounters. Walking around the block, you turn a corner and there's a dog in your face. You enter your vet's waiting room with your dog after carefully scoping out the territory. Just as you settle into your seat, the door opens from the exam room area and an exuberant Labrador Retriever comes flying through, towing his owner at the end of a retractable leash. Help!

Evasive action techniques

You can practice several exercises to prepare for encounters that need evasive action:

- **Emergency Exit:** Practice a "turn and run away" maneuver in non-emergency times. Teach your dog a cue, such as "Run away!" that means "Let's run the other way very fast." To teach this, say your cue, then turn quickly, inviting your dog to run with you. Make fun noises, pat your leg, toss a favorite toy in the new direction—anything to get the dog excited about running with you. Make it fun, so when you walk around the corner and see the other dog, your dog hears the cue, gets happy and spins on his heel to run away with you—before he has time to react to the presence of the other dog.
- **Targeting.** Teach your dog to touch his nose to a designated target—your fist or the palm of your hand—on cue. Offer your palm or closed fist to the dog at nose level, and when he sniffs it, Click! a clicker or say "Yes!" and then feed him a yummy treat. If he doesn't sniff your hand, smear a tiny dab of baby food or squeeze cheese on it to get him started. When he'll touch your hand with his nose consistently every time you offer it, start saying "Touch!" just before he connects. Practice until he bumps his nose into your hand solidly every time.

Dogs tend to love targeting. Get yours so happy about targeting that you can use it to keep his attention focused on you—instead of on the other dog in the veterinary waiting room. (Note: this is a management strategy, not to be confused with or take the place of good behavior modification using counter-conditioning, in which you *want* your dog to look at the other dog.)

- **Watch Me:** Teach this cue—or a similar one—to mean "Make eye contact with me and keep making eye contact with me." You can just Click! the clicker or say "Yes!" and then feed a treat whenever your dog makes eye contact with you. If you reinforce the behavior often, your dog will start offering it on purpose. Then you can add your "Watch me!" cue. Or you can move a treat toward your eyes to lure eye contact, adding the cue and fading the use of the lure when he starts offering eye contact. Again, this puts your dog's attention and focus on you instead of on the other dog. If your dog is still sub-threshold but not giving you a CER, you may be able to interrupt his increasing arousal by having him look at you.
- **Tug of War:** Dogs can concentrate on only one thing at a time. If you teach your dog to play a low-key game of tug, you may be able to occupy his brain with the sight of his beloved tug toy when another dog arrives unexpectedly on the scene. Use a long, soft braided rope tug toy to keep dog teeth far from human skin. Offer the toy and say "Take it!" Let him grab it, resist gently while saying the cue "Tug!" and then trade him a treat for the toy with the cue "Give!" Be sure to keep it low-key. A high-arousal all-out game of tug will only serve to feed his reactivity.

Often, a client who comes to me with a dog-reactive dog has already tried a variety of other approaches to modifying the behavior—many of which actually have exacerbated the behavior rather than decreasing it. Old-fashioned training methods that advocate the use of pain and force to dominate the dog and suppress unwanted behaviors are not appropriate in general, and are particularly inappropriate with aggression-related behaviors. They're likely to worsen the behavior—give the dog an escalated negative association with the presence of other dogs.

Tools and techniques I urge you *not* to use with your dog-reactive dog include prong and electronic shock collars; spray bottles; scruff shakes; **flooding**, which entails presenting the stimulus—other dogs—at full intensity until your dog gives up and shuts down; and verbal and physical corrections. While considerably gentler than the inhumane techniques I've just described, even relatively mild corrections can increase your dog's stress around other dogs and be counterproductive to your behavior modification program.

If you are the owner of a reactive dog, don't despair. With some effort, most dogs can be improved, some to normal or near-normal behavior. I have numerous clients who are now competing and winning in a variety of dog sports with their previously reactive dogs, and many others who are happy that they can now simply walk their dogs around the block without drama or struggle.

CHAPTER 17

Idiopathic Aggression

"Rage syndrome." The term conjures up mental images of a Cujo-dog, running around terrorizing the countryside. If you're the owner of a dog who suffers from it, it's almost that bad—never knowing when your beloved pal is going to turn suddenly, without warning, into a biting, raging canine tornado.

The condition commonly known as rage syndrome is actually more appropriately called **idiopathic** aggression. The dictionary definition of idiopathic is: "Of, relating to, or designating a disease having no known cause." It applies perfectly to this behavior, which has confounded behaviorists for decades. Many behavior professionals urge that the use of the term "rage syndrome" be discontinued. The word "rage" implies some emotional cause in response to an identifiable and consistent stimulus or combination of stimuli, which should logically lend itself to modification through desensitization and counter-conditioning. Idiopathic aggression doesn't. It is an extremely difficult and heartbreaking condition to deal with.

Earmarks of idiopathic aggression

Most behavior professionals agree that the following are the earmarks of idiopathic aggression:

- No identifiable trigger stimulus/stimuli
- Intense, explosive aggression
- Onset most commonly reported in dogs one to three years old

Some owners report that their dogs get a glazed or "possessed" look in their eyes just prior to an idiopathic outburst, or act confused. Certain breeds seem more prone to suffer from this condition, including Cocker and Springer Spaniels (hence the once-common terms Spaniel rage, Cocker rage and Springer rage), Bernese Mountain Dogs, St. Bernards, Doberman Pinschers, German Shepherds and Lhasa Apsos. This would suggest a likely genetic component to the problem.

The good news is that true idiopathic aggression is also a particularly uncommon condition. Discussed and studied widely in the 1970s and 80s, it captured the imagination of the dog world, and soon every dog with episodes of sudden, explosive aggression was tagged with the unfortunate "rage syndrome" label, especially if it was a Spaniel of any type. We have since come to our senses, and now investigate much more carefully before concluding that there is truly "no known cause" for a dog's aggression and that the dog has idiopathic aggression.

A thorough exploration of the dog's behavior history and owner's observations often can ferret out explainable causes for the aggression. The appropriate diagnosis often turns out to be impulse control aggression (once widely known as "dominance aggression") and/or resource guarding—both of which can also generate very violent, explosive reactions.

An owner can easily miss her dog's warning signs prior to an impulse control attack, especially if the warning signs have been suppressed by prior physical or verbal punishment. While some dogs' lists of guardable resources may be limited and precise, with others it can be difficult to identify and recognize a resource that a dog has determined to be valuable and worth guarding. The glazed look reported by some owners may also be their interpretation of the "hard stare" or "freeze" that many dogs give as a warning signal just prior to an attack.

Different behavior professionals have used and continue to use different terms for what was once more commonly known as "rage syndrome," even though "idiopathic aggression" is now more commonly accepted despite its uncertain cause. A variety of studies and testing over the past 30 years have failed to produce a clear cause or a definitive diagnosis for idiopathic aggression. So even though behavior professionals can't even agree on what to call it, you may hear these terms:

- **Rage syndrome:** This once popular term has fallen into disfavor, due to its overuse, misuse and poor characterization of the actual condition
- **Low-threshold dominance aggression:** Favored by those who hold that idiopathic aggression is actually a manifestation of status-related aggression with very subtle triggers
- **Mental lapse aggression syndrome:** Attached to cases diagnosed as a result of certain electroencephalogram readings (low-voltage, fast activity)
- **Stimulus responsive psychomotor epilepsy:** Favored by some who suspect that idiopathic aggression is actually epileptic seizure activity

Possible causes

Although the true cause of idiopathic aggression is still not understood, and behaviorists each tend to defend their "favorite" theories, there is universal agreement that it is a very rare condition, and one that is extremely difficult to treat. Given the failure to find a specific cause, it is quite possible that there are multiple different causes for unexplainable aggressive behaviors that are all grouped under the term "idiopathic aggression." Some dogs in the midst of an episode may be foaming at the mouth and twitching, which could be an indication of epileptic seizures. The most common onset of the behavior between one and three years of age also coincides with the appearance of most impulse control aggression, as well as the development of idiopathic epilepsy, making it even impossible to use age of onset as a differential diagnosis.

Some researchers have produced abnormal electroencephalogram readings in some dogs suspected of having idiopathic aggression, but not all such dogs they studied. Other researchers have been unable to reproduce even those inconclusive results.

Another theory is that the behavior is caused by damage to the area of the brain responsible for aggressive behavior. Yet another is that it is actually a manifestation of impulse control aggression triggered by very subtle stimuli. Clearly, we just don't know.

The fact that idiopathic aggression by definition cannot be induced also makes it difficult to study and even try to find answers to the question of cause. Unlike a behavior like resource guarding—which is easy to induce and therefore easy to study in a clinical setting—the very nature of idiopathic aggression dictates that it cannot be reproduced or studied at will.

Treatment

Without knowing the cause of idiopathic aggression, treatment is difficult and frequently unsuccessful. The condition is also virtually impossible to manage safely because of the sheer unpredictability of the outbursts. Prognosis, unfortunately, is very poor, and many dogs with true idiopathic aggression must be euthanized, for the safety of surrounding humans.

Don't despair, however, if someone has told you your dog has "rage syndrome." First of all, he probably doesn't. Remember, the condition is extremely rare, and the label still gets applied all too often by uneducated dog folk to canines whose aggressive behaviors are perfectly explainable by a more knowledgeable observer. Your first step is to find a skilled and positive trainer/behavior consultant who can give you a more educated analysis of your dog's aggression. A good behavior modification program applied by a committed owner in consultation with a capable behavior professional can succeed in decreasing and/or resolving many aggression cases, and help you devise appropriate management plans where necessary, to keep family members, friends and visitors safe.

If your behavior professional also believes that you have a rare case of idiopathic aggression on your hands, then a trip to a veterinary behaviorist is in order. Some dogs will respond to drug therapies for this condition—many will not. Some minor success has been reported with the administration of phenobarbital, but it is unclear as to whether the results are from the sedative effect of the drug, or if there is an actual therapeutic effect.

In many cases of true idiopathic aggression, euthanasia is the only solution. Because the aggressive explosions are truly violent and totally unpredictable, it is neither safe nor fair to expose yourself or friends and family to the potentially disfiguring, even deadly, results of such an attack. If this is the sad conclusion in the case of your dog, comfort yourself with the knowledge that you have done everything humanly possible for him, hold him close as you say good-bye and send him gently to a safer place. Then remember to take good care of yourself.

CHAPTER 18

Professionals: Finding One/Being One

For the final three chapters I am going to switch gears away from management and modification strategies you can implement yourself, in recognition that the aggression problems you face may require the help of a professional. A listing of certifications and organizations to help you locate the right professional for your dog is included in the Appendix.

Evaluating trainers and behaviorists

If do you need help, the dog training and behavior profession boasts a mind-boggling panoply of credentials—some of them more meaningful than others. You may be surprised to discover that there are *no* educational, experience, training, skill, certification or licensing requirements for *anyone* to call themselves a dog trainer or behaviorist in the United States. None. Zip. Zero. Nada. Your plumber could decide to hang out a shingle and start training dogs tomorrow, even if he or she has never touched or even seen a dog in his or her entire life. Shocking, isn't it?

There are certainly scores of excellent educational *opportunities* for animal training and behavior professionals to increase their skills and knowledge, and to be fair, many do attend courses and seek various kinds of certification in the field. However, short of a possible town or county ordinance that may have some professional requirements (we were unable to find any, but aren't ruling out the possibility), a trainer can pretty much call herself almost anything she wants, and do almost anything to her clients' dogs in the name of training and behavior modification, even in the complete absence of any education or credentials whatsoever.

In fact, the number of truly qualified, well-educated training and behavior professionals has exploded since the 1990s, and there is growing agreement among *ethical* behavior and training professionals that the actual term "behaviorist" *should* be reserved for those in the field who have advanced degrees in behavior and/or veterinary medicine and behavior. Those who don't have such degrees and who wish to show respect to degreed behaviorists use terms like "behavior consultant," "behavior counselor" and "behavior professional" to describe what they do. That said, plenty of people who offer services in training and behavior totally disregard that courtesy. The media rarely get it right—calling anyone they interview who has anything to do with training animals a "behaviorist." And the general public pretty much doesn't have a clue that there's a difference.

In addition, there are widely diverse philosophies about dog training and behavior modification methods. I heartily endorse courses and certifications that follow a force-free, positive reinforcement–based philosophy, and urge you to avoid those that espouse the use of tools and methods that involve the deliberate application of force, coercion, pain, discomfort and/or intimidation. In the Appendix, I have provided a list of professional organizations, certifying bodies, and schools and courses for dog behavior professionals.

On selecting your competent behavior professional

It pays to remember that this field is a caveat emptor world, and you would do well to research the credentials of any and all training and behavior professionals, whether they bear an impressive set of letters behind their names or not. Then interview them. Ask about their methods and philosophies. Ask for references. Find out how long they've been practicing. Read their website, blogs and articles to see if what they publish about their work is congruent with what they are telling you. Only commit to working with a professional who has solid credentials, is committed to modern, science-based, force-free methods, and whose personal style you are comfortable with. Dog training and behavior professionals should be as gentle and positive with their human clients as they are with their canine clients. No matter how well you have pre-screened your professional, be prepared to intervene if at any time they try to do anything with your dog that makes you uncomfortable. Trust your instincts.

On being a competent canine behavior professional

If you are already a behavior professional working with aggression cases or are hoping to become one, it is critically important that you act ethically. Despite the fact that there are no credentials required by law or educational standards you must meet in most places in the United States, ethics demand that you have them. (Note that ethical standards I recommend for professional trainers can be used to evaluate anyone you may choose to hire as well.)

As you will see in the Appendix, your choice of credentialing is broad. You can go the college degree route, or select one of the less formal but still rigorous courses of study offered online or hands-on. When you are ready, determine which certifying organization is the right fit for you.

You will need experience in addition to any of the credentialing choices. Look for internships or apprenticeships with an established, credentialed behavior professional whom you admire, and with whom you are philosophically congruent. Offer to be the leader for a 4-H Dog Project. Volunteer to work with dogs at a shelter or rescue group under a qualified mentor. A shelter is a fantastic place to gain experience—you will see a variety of dogs and behaviors all in one place that it would take you decades to encounter otherwise—and there's no owner looking over your shoulder—only your mentor.

When you believe you are ready to offer aggression-modification services, do a reality check with other professionals who know you. If they agree that you are ready, start small. Advise potential clients that you are relatively new to the aggression field, and that you will be happy to do an initial consult to determine if you can help them or if you need to refer to someone more experienced. If you get a Teddie or a Helga—a dog who just needs his owners to behave differently—dive in. If you realize the case is beyond your skillset, have a list of possible referrals already in hand to give the client. Then ask if they are comfortable having you attend the referrals session with them—a great way to gain additional experience. Any trainer who refers to me is welcome to sit in on the consult—in part because I want to support and help them further their education, and in part because I often send the client back home with their modification program and the hope that the referring trainer can continue to work with them at home.

Even if you take on a case that you believe is appropriate for your level of skill and experience, you may reach a point in your relationship with that client where you realize they need more help than you can offer. Do not hesitate to refer a client when you realize their dog's behavior challenge is beyond your skill set. I have referred several clients on to veterinary behaviorists over the years, and they almost always get referred back for assistance in implementing the program the veterinary behaviorist has recommended. Referring is the professional, ethical and right thing to do. Failing to refer a case that is beyond your depth is unethical, unprofessional and dangerous.

CHAPTER 19

Rehoming Responsibly

A client sent me an email yesterday to tell me that she has been unable to implement our agreed-upon behavior modification program due to the full-time responsibility of caring for an elderly parent. She is looking to rehome her dog. Bailey, an otherwise delightful one-year-old Labrador Retriever, has mild-to-moderate dog-reactive/aggressive behavior, as well as the high energy level typical of an adolescent Lab. Barb has been bringing him to Peaceable Paws since puppy class. I was saddened to hear she was giving him up. It's always tragic for a dog, and the humans who know him, when the promise of a lifelong loving home falls through.

Ask any animal shelter or rescue group, and they will tell you that owners surrender their dogs for a myriad of reasons. Common ones include: moving—can't keep, landlord won't allow, not enough time, and can't afford.

Every day thousands of dog lovers move and take their dogs with them, find a new place to live where dogs are allowed, rearrange busy schedules to make time for their dogs, and reprioritize budgets to cover the expense of caring for their canines. Animal protection and rescue workers often become cynical about and unsympathetic toward those who give up their dogs. Many of us who love our dogs find it difficult to imagine any legitimate reason for giving them up.

Every dog deserves a lifelong loving home with his own humans, his own sofa and maybe his own cat.

When to consider rehoming

While it's true that many dogs are given up for seemingly frivolous reasons, there are times when it is the right thing to do.

The dog is a danger to someone in the household, or to the community. This often entails aggressive behavior, but not always. Sometimes an aging dog lover makes the mistake of replacing her beloved senior dog who recently passed away with a puppy of the same breed, forgetting that she was 15 years younger and sprier the last time she had a bouncing adolescent 80-pound canine underfoot. If the human's dexterity and balance is beginning to fail her, and/or if she is physically unable to meet the dog's activity needs, rehoming may be the best option. While daycare and pet walkers may be able to help with some of the exercise, it may still present too great a threat to her safety. If that's the case, rehoming is the right choice.

A rowdy dog may also present some physical risk to small children in the home. Good management can often minimize the danger while the child grows and the dog gets trained. Aggression, however, is another matter.

Aggression alone is not necessarily a reason to give up your dog. It is irresponsible parenting and dog owning, however, to keep a dog who shows a willingness to bite kids in a home with children. Dogs who live in homes with small children must adore them, or the child's safety is at significant risk. Anything less than "adore" suggests the dog should be rehomed, or at least sent off to stay with relatives until the child is old enough to no longer be at risk, and/or the dog has learned to love children. It's a lot easier to rehome a dog *before* he bites a child…

A dog with aggressive behaviors presents a risk to the community if the owner is unwilling or unable to take necessary management steps to keep the community—and the dog—safe. While this can be due to a lack of concern on the owner's part, it can also be a result of denial and/or lack of education. When aggressive behaviors have been identified in a dog, it is critically important that the owners prevent the dog from having any opportunity to bite, and that they seek assistance from a qualified force-free behavior professional for help in managing and modifying the behavior.

An unavoidable change in life circumstances precludes keeping the dog. Stuff happens. Beatle John Lennon once sang, "Life is what happens when you're busy making other plans." It's all too true. You may have the strongest commitment in the world to your dog, but if life circumstances change and you can truly no longer care for him, then rehoming is the responsible decision. I'm not talking about simple priority choices (we can't afford the dog's ACL surgery because we want to go to Europe this summer); I'm talking about unavoidable life events such as heart attacks, strokes, foreclosure, moving to a long-term care facility and other life-shattering occurrences. Sometimes, tragically, you really can't care for your beloved canine any longer.

The dog has a health or behavior problem that is beyond the means of the owner to resolve. Quality of life is an important consideration for dogs *and* humans. If you really can't afford care that your dog needs, you either provide it anyway, perhaps at the cost of your own health or diet, or you don't provide it and your dog suffers. You can choose to make sacrifices in order to provide for your beloved dog, but there may come a legitimate time when the sacrifice is too great, or the challenge too difficult. Some medical procedures now available for dogs cost tens of thousands of dollars. Just because we *can* fix something and prolong life doesn't always mean we *should.* A loving owner may be completely willing to work with her difficult dog's behaviors, but physically unable to do so. In those cases, rehoming or even euthanasia may well be the best choice. Behavior challenges in addition to aggression that can be extremely difficult to live with include severe separation anxiety and a variety of canine compulsive disorders. While these sometimes respond to treatment, often with the help of behavior modification drugs, they don't always, and quality of life is greatly damaged for both dog and owner.

Options for rehoming

We live in a society where there are far more dogs than there are homes that are looking for dogs. This can make it a challenging proposition to rehome a dog, especially one with major health or behavior problems. Here are options to consider when you must give up your dog:

1. **Return her to the breeder, shelter or rescue group you acquired her from.** Responsible breeders and adoption organizations often contractually require this, although some may allow you to rehome to someone you know that they pre-approve. Caveats: If the place where you got your dog was less-than-reputable—overcrowded, poor conditions—you won't want to return the dog there. If you got her from a pet store or puppy mill, returning is not an option.

2. **Place her with a trusted friend or family member.** Well-loved, well-behaved, healthy dogs usually have a circle of admirers who would jump at the chance to adopt. Caveats: Even your best friend or favorite relative may decline to take on a dog with major health or behavior challenges. You must be honest about these challenges. Full disclosure is imperative. Also, talk with your attorney—you may still bear some liability if you rehome your dog and he bites someone in the future.

3. **Advertise for someone to adopt her.** Caveats: It's not easy to screen potential adopters—you risk placing your dog with someone who won't provide the kind of loving care you want for her, despite their assurances. This goes triple if there are health or behavior issues. Never advertise a dog for free, especially on an internet site. Prospective adopters may seem to be animal lovers when they contact you, but stories abound about people who do bad things with free dogs, ranging from not providing the housing, love and care they promised, to using them as bait dogs for dog fighting, or even flipping them (selling them for a higher price to someone else and making a hearty profit off of your precious pet).

4. **Take her to a good shelter or rescue.** There are thousands of excellent dog adoption services around the country. Many provide medical treatment that owners couldn't afford for at least some of the dogs in their care. The best have behavior departments or at least working relationships with qualified professionals to modify difficult behaviors in order to make dogs more likely to succeed in their next, hopefully final, homes—but many will *not* take a dog with a history of aggressive behavior. Not everything is fixable, and responsible groups still have to make difficult euthanasia decisions, but your dog might be one they can help. Caveats: Be sure you research these groups diligently. Visit the facility to see that it's clean and well-run. If you can't visit, don't leave your dog there. If your dog isn't adopted, she may suffer in a cage at a "no-kill" shelter for the rest of her life, or worse, in the hands of a hoarder posing as a shelter or rescue. Again, you must be brutally honest about your dog's health or behavior problems.

An ethical, reputable breeder, shelter or rescue group won't rehome a dog with aggressive behaviors unless they can do behavior modification to make the dog safe, or place him with full disclosure in an experienced home capable of doing needed management and modification. Needless to say, those homes are hard to come by.

5. **Have her euthanized.** As impossibly painful as this decision is for you to make, it may be the kindest thing you can do, especially if your dog has significant health and/or behavior issues. You love her, and can't muster the resources to give her what she needs. It may not be realistic to ask someone else to care for her, and she could be abused or neglected in the process. Dying peacefully in the arms of someone who loves her is better than dying neglected in someone's back yard. When I have a client considering this option because of difficult canine behaviors, I gently suggest that euthanasia is not an inappropriate choice for a loved dog if the client is unable to do the things necessary to restore her dog to physical health, or to manage and/or modify behaviors. I don't tell her she should make that choice, but I let her know I'll support her if she does.

Any one of these decisions, especially the last, can be irrevocable. Be sure you've thought it through carefully, and truly exhausted all your options for fulfilling the commitment you made to your dog when you adopted her, before giving her up. You don't want this to be a decision you regret for the rest of your life—and hers.

Oh, by the way, I received another email from Barb this morning. A family decision to place the parent in a long-term care facility has given Barb new resources, new energy and a renewed commitment to work with Bailey. For now, he's staying in his home. Cross your fingers.

CHAPTER 20

Be Your Dog's Advocate

You are your dog's advocate and protector. He depends on you to keep him safe in this world. All too often, however, the owner abdicates that role, and the dog discovers he must protect himself. Voilà—aggression, in all the manifestations already presented here in prior chapters.

The better you are at fulfilling your role as protector and advocate, the less likely your dog will feel the need to protect himself from the world around him. How wonderful for you *and* your dog if you do such a great job of convincing him that the world is a safe and happy place that he *never* feels the need to growl, snarl, snap or bite.

As your dog's advocate, you gently prevent him from getting himself into dangerous situations, and you assertively prevent others from doing harm to him. I vividly remember an incident, many decades ago when I was still a sweet young thing just learning how to assert myself in the world. I was at a party with my adolescent Australian Kelpie, Keli, who was on track to become a canine field agent with me in my role as a humane officer/animal control officer for the Marin Humane Society in Novato, California. An exceedingly intoxicated party-goer kept teasing Keli, and I had politely asked him twice to leave her alone, but he persisted. Finally pushed over *my* threshold I marched up to him, grabbed both his arms and in his face yelled, "I told you to quit f****** with her! Now leave her the f*** alone!" He did.

One common scenario requiring your advocacy skills involves the person who is sure she is the answer to every dog's ills. You see her approaching your stranger-aggressive dog with "that look" in her eyes. You step forward and say politely, "Please stop. My dog isn't comfortable with strangers."

"Oh, it's okay," she assures you, "dogs love me." She proceeds toward you.

Perfect recipe for a dog bite. In an instant you must become Assertive Annie and drop all pretense of being polite. "Stop!" you announce loudly, and hold up your hand like a traffic cop. If necessary, then you do an Emergency Escape—give your "Run Away" cue, turn and dash off with your dog who is now happily anticipating the fun party at the end of your escape run, instead of stressing at the approach of a stranger. Phew! Dodged that bullet! If it's a neighbor, relative or acquaintance whom you have just offended, you can apologize and explain later, after your dog is safe at home.

It can be even more difficult to be your dog's champion when it involves your animal care professionals—trainers, groomers, even veterinarians—people you are paying and want to trust to give you good advice and information. I tell my clients, "I don't care *who* it is—even if it's me...if someone tries to do something to your dog that you are not comfortable with, you have the right and the obligation to stop them."

Veterinarians can be a significant challenge. It is common procedure in many veterinary practices to remove the dog to a back room for even simple procedures such as vaccinations. Not only do I not allow my dogs' veterinarians to do that, there are a number of other vet clinic scenarios where I insist on calling the shots (no pun intended).

Here are some examples of situations where you can, and have every right to, intervene on your dog's behalf:

1. **Stay in the room:** Some vets insist that their clients' difficult dogs are better behaved when the owner isn't present. They have the tech whisk the dog to a back room where the vet does whatever needs to be done, then return the dog to the owner, claiming the dog was "fine." While it is possible that some dogs are calmer when not in the presence of a stressed owner, there are several other explanations for this, none of them acceptable:

    i. A fearful dog may, indeed, shut down when taken away from the owner. While a shut-down dog may be easier for the vet and her staff to handle, it is likely that the dog is becoming more stressed and fearful during the procedure, and will then be even more stressed (and harder to handle) the next time he needs to be examined, vaccinated or treated, by the owner as well as the veterinarian.

    ii. When the owner's not there to watch, vets and clinic staff may be less inhibited about using significant force to compel the dog to accept the handling. In extreme cases, some veterinarians have even been caught on video hitting dogs and worse, throwing them against a wall in response to their resistance. If you are there, they are likely to at least moderate their use of force.

iii. When the owner is there, not only might the clinic staff feel less free to use forcible restraint methods they "know" will work, they also may have to explain and defend what they are doing, or risk upsetting the owner and losing a client.

2. **Ask for sedation:** For the dog, not for you...although some owners might benefit from a little medication as well. If your dog is resisting to the point your veterinarian feels inclined to use forcible restraint, ask that she use drugs instead. Unless there is a medical reason preventing your dog from being sedated, this is a far easier, less stressful solution for all concerned, both human and canine. Yes, it will cost you a little more, and yes, there is a slight risk, even for a healthy dog, but well worth both, in my eyes. Please note: Many veterinarians administer acepromazine as a sedative when clients request medication. Dr. Karen Overall vehemently argues against the use of acepromazine for dogs. She says, "I know that the common 'treatment' for storm and noise phobias and veterinary office visits is acepromazine. In truth, I wish this medication would be placed at the far back of a top shelf and used only exceptionally. Acepromazine is a dissociative anesthetic meaning that it scrambles perceptions. Ask yourself if a scrambling of perceptions will make an anxious or uncertain dog worse or better." If your vet agrees to sedate your dog, ask what drug she plans to use. If she suggests "ace" for your dog, ask her to watch this video of Dr. Overall speaking about acepromazine: *www.youtube.com/watch?v=6-GsmrFYHKk,* and/or ask her to speak with a veterinary behaviorist to determine what might be the most appropriate drug for your dog for this situation.

   (Note: If you do get very stressed about taking your dog to the vet, you may want to ask a trusted friend/advocate to take her for you, and stay with her. Overwrought owners who freak their dogs out at the vet are not helping the staff or, more importantly, their dogs, by being present with that type of energy.)

3. **Intervene as needed:** One of the reasons some vets prefer not to have owners present is that if the dog does continue to resist, they may opt to use restraint methods that many owners would find appalling and unacceptable. In the vets' defense, they have a job to do, and muzzling and forcible restraint enable them to get the job done while ensuring their own safety and the safety of their staff. It also ensures that your dog's behavior will likely get worse and worse with each subsequent visit to the vet clinic. However, most vet office procedures are not urgent, and if your vet explains what she needs to be able to do, you could conceivably go home with a behavior modification protocol that will, in a reasonable amount of time, enable you to bring your dog back for the next

appointment, willing and able to tolerate routine veterinary procedures. Unless your dog is bleeding to death from a severed artery or suffering from some other dire, life-threatening emergency, make it clear to your vet that you won't tolerate the use of force, and ask her to work with you to find alternatives. Be prepared to assertively stop clinic staff from doing anything to your dog that you are not comfortable with.

4. **Choose your surface:** Some dogs do great on the exam table—but even better if you bring a soft, familiar rug or blanket, memory-foam bathmat, rubberized cabinet liner or non-slip rug sheeting from home to put on it so it's not so shiny, slippery or scary. Other dogs do much better on the floor of the exam room. Stress causes aggression, so if you know that your dog will be less stressed on the floor than on the table, talk your vet into doing the exam and procedures, whenever possible, on the down-low.

5. **Feed treats:** I recently had to take our 12-year-old Cardigan Corgi, Lucy, to our vet for an anal gland exam (due to excessive licking and scooting). I was a little apprehensive, as Lucy has, in the past, been clear about her discomfort with vet exams. I was seeing a new vet at Longmeadow Animal Hospital, and had no idea what to expect. Girding my advocacy loins for battle, I walked Lucy into the exam room, and immediately started feeding treats to "prime" her (get her in a happy frame of mind) for the exam. To my delight, Dr. Skopets didn't suggest they take Lucy to a back room, so I didn't have to fight that battle. And when I advised him that she had been difficult in the past and would be happier if I fed her while he examined her, he said, "Well then, you just keep right on feeding her."

Fortunately, the world of dog care and training seems to be moving slowly but inexorably in a more positive direction. There is a gentle breeze of change wafting through the veterinary community, led by noted veterinary behaviorists Dr. Karen Overall and the late Dr. Sophia Yin, and veterinarian Dr. Marty Becker. All three of these veterinarians have long been outspoken advocates for a kinder, gentler approach to handling animals at veterinary clinics, to combat the widespread challenge of dogs (and other animal companions) who become increasingly fearful, difficult to handle and even seriously aggressive with repeated visits to the animal doctor. Dr. Becker is spearheading an effort entitled "Fear-Free Veterinary Visits" that educates veterinarians about how to make veterinary visits and procedures less aversive to their furred and feathered clients. (Ask your vet if she is involved!) There are studies, too, that confirm the negative effects of the use of coercion and pain in dog training and handling procedures, and verify the effectiveness of positive reinforcement–based techniques.

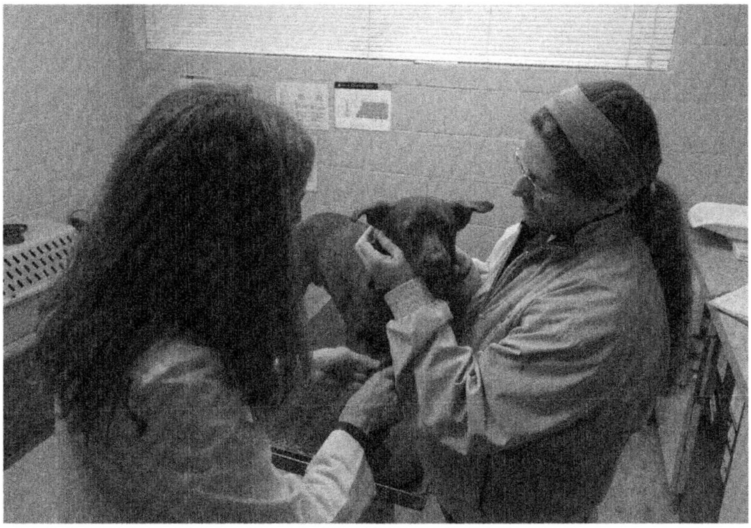

Author Pat Miller reassures her slightly worried Australian Kelpie, Kaizen, while he is being examined by his veterinarian, Dr. Tracy Barlup. Note the non-slip pad on the exam table.

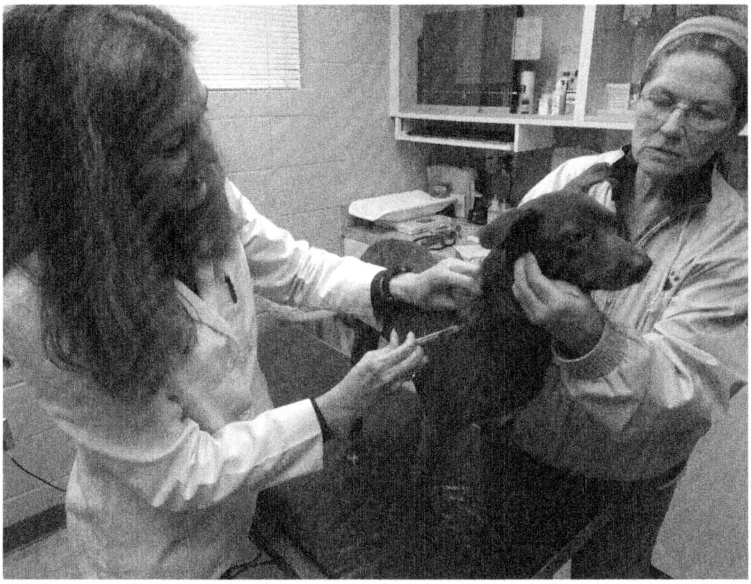

And lightly restrains him for his vaccination (the best restraint is the least restraint).

Twenty years ago when my Peaceable Paws training and behavior business was new, prospective clients never asked about our training methods or philosophy. Today we routinely get calls from clients who inquire first, prior to making the decision to choose us as their service provider. Twenty years ago you would have been hard pressed to find a force-free training and behavior professional in your community. Today, chances are there is at least one within reasonable driving distance of you.

All of this bodes well for the future of our relationships with our dogs. Yes, we can modify aggressive behavior, but how lovely it would be to see the day when it isn't necessary to do so, because our species has learned how to live in peaceful harmony with our four-legged best friends.

Meanwhile…go be your dog's unabashed advocate. Protect him, manage his environment and help him learn how to live in an aggression-free world. His life depends on it. He's counting on you.

APPENDIX

Where to Find Professional Help

Anybody can print up a business card and claim to be an expert canine behaviorist or dog trainer specializing in behavior problems. And if they charge you money—and you pay them—then they are professionals, right? Fortunately in recent years a number of professional organizations have arisen that certify that people taking their courses and graduating from their programs are qualified to help you deal with your dog's problem behaviors.

The true behaviorists

- **DACVB:** There are three exceptions to the behaviorist titling free-for-all I discussed in Chapter 18. At the top of the behaviorist food chain is the veterinary behaviorist—the DACVB. In order to call oneself a *veterinary* behaviorist, one must, of course, be a veterinarian, and then meet the rigorous qualifications set by the American College of Veterinary Behavior (ACVB) and pass the two-day veterinary board exam in behavior. The American College of Veterinary Behaviorists is a professional organization of veterinarians who are board certified in the specialty of veterinary behavior. Board-certified specialists are known as diplomates (diplomates of the ACVB = DACVB). One who calls himself a veterinary behaviorist without this credential is practicing veterinary behavioral medicine without a license and is subject to prosecution. The general requirements include: complete the equivalent of an internship; complete a conforming residency at an approved university program such as the University of California-Davis, Tufts University and the University of Pennsylvania, or a non-conforming training program that was mentored and approved by ACVB; accomplish a supervised behavioral caseload (the first 25 clinical cases are seen with the mentor present, 25 of the next 50 cases are seen under the direct supervision of the mentor, close supervision is required for the first 200 cases);

author a scientific paper published in a peer-reviewed journal based on the candidate's own research; write three peer-reviewed case reports; and successfully complete a comprehensive two-day board exam. When that examination has been successfully completed, the individual may become an ACVB diplomate. As of January 2016, there were a total of 70 DACVBs in the world, 61 of those in the United States. (Other countries may have other designations for their equivalent of the DACVB.)

- **CAAB:** Next in line is the Certified Applied Animal Behaviorist (CAAB). In order to become a CAAB, one must meet the qualifications set by the Animal Behavior Society (ABS). ABS requirements include: Obtain a PhD (doctoral degree) in a biological or behavioral science with an emphasis on animal behavior, including five years of professional experience; or a doctorate in veterinary medicine plus two years in a university-approved residency in animal behavior, and three additional years of professional experience in applied animal behavior; demonstrate a thorough knowledge of the literature, scientific principles and principles of animal behavior; submit original contributions or original interpretations of animal behavior information; show evidence of significant experience working interactively with a particular species as a researcher or research assistant, or intern with a Certified Applied Animal Behaviorist prior to working independently with the species in a clinical animal behavior setting; attend and present a contributed talk or poster at an ABS annual meeting prior to applying for certification; and meet all the requirements for an Associate Certified Applied Animal Behaviorist (see next).

Animal Behavior Society

- **ACAAB:** The ACAAB is on the next rung down the ladder. Don't let the "associate" fool you—requirements for this level of certification are still stringent: First, obtain a master's degree from an accredited college or university in a biological or behavioral science with an emphasis in animal behavior. The degree should include a research-based thesis. Coursework must include 30 semester credits in behavioral science courses, including nine semester credits in ethology, animal behavior and/or comparative psychology, and nine semester credits in animal learning, conditioning and/or animal psychology. Next, provide evidence of a minimum of two years of professional experience in applied animal behavior; show evidence of significant experience working interactively with a particular species (such as a researcher, research assistant or intern working with a Certified Applied Animal Behaviorist) prior to working independently with the species in a clinical animal behavior setting; attend and present a contributed talk or poster at an ABS annual meeting prior to applying for certification;

provide a minimum of three letters of recommendation, one from a certified ABS member and one from a regular ABS member affirming the applicant's professional experience in the areas listed above. As of January 2016, there are a total of 47 CAABs and ACAABs combined.

Other training and behavior associations

- **APDT:** The Association of Professional Dog Trainers. With fewer than 100 certified behaviorists in the entire United States (many of whom do *not* work with companion animals), the dog population would be seriously underserved if there were no other qualified behavior and training professionals to be found. Recognizing the desperate need for professionalism in the field, British veterinary behaviorist Ian Dunbar founded the Association of Pet Dog Trainers in 1991 (recently renamed the Association of Professional Dog Trainers) as a forum for trainers to network with each other and provide educational opportunities. The APDT held its first annual educational conference in Orlando, Florida, in 1993, and in 2010 declared January to be *National Train Your Dog Month.* The annual conference continues to this day, joined by frequent online webinar offerings. While the APDT itself does not certify trainers, nor are its members necessarily committed to force-free training, this organization did launch the CCPDT in 2001 (see below), which certifies more than 2,000 training and behavior professionals worldwide and requires that its certificants follow a humane hierarchy when using training tools and methods. Today, with more than 5,000 members, the APDT is the largest dog training organization in the world. There are also APDTs in the United Kingdom, Canada, Australia and New Zealand.

Association of Professional Dog Trainers

- **AVSAB:** The American Veterinary Society of Animal Behavior (AVSAB) is a group of veterinarians and research professionals who share an interest in understanding behavior in animals. Founded in 1976, AVSAB is committed to improving the quality of life of all animals and strengthening the bond between animals and their owners. Membership in this organization is open to all veterinarians, veterinary students and non-veterinarians who have a PhD in animal behavior or a closely related field. AVSAB membership is *not* a certification, and is not a statement of member skills or qualifications in behavior work.

American Veterinary Society of Animal Behavior

- **CCPDT:** The Certification Council for Professional Dog Trainers' certification program was the first national certification for dog trainers in the United States. Until the creation of the CCPDT in 2001, there was no nationally available certification process for dog trainers in this country. Unlike many other certifications, CCPDT tests are monitored, and the testing processes are standardized. The CCPDT administered its first test September 28, 2001, during the Association of Pet Dog Trainers (APDT) annual educational conference in Ellenville, New York. Today the CCPDT boasts more than 2,000 certificants in three categories worldwide, and is working on a fourth certificate category. CCPDT requires its certificants to abide by a code of ethics and adhere to a humane hierarchy in their behavior and training practices. CCPDT is not a membership organization; you do not join in order to become a certificant.

  Certification Council for Professional Dog Trainers

    - **CPDT-KA:** The Certified Professional Dog Trainer-Knowledge Assessed must pass a comprehensive written exam, submit confirmation of at least 300 hours of experience in dog training within the past five years, have a high school diploma or GED equivalent, and submit three references (from a veterinarian, a dog training client and a colleague in the behavior and training profession).

    - **CPDT-KSA:** The Certified Professional Dog Trainer-Knowledge and Skills Assessed must hold a CPDT-KA credential and additionally pass a video skills examination of him or herself training four different skills as designated by the CCPDT, one skill each to four different dogs not living with or previously trained by the candidate.

    - **CBCC-KA:** The Certified Behavior Consultant, Canine-Knowledge Assessed must pass a comprehensive written exam; submit records of 500 hours in canine behavior consulting on fear, phobias, compulsive behaviors, anxiety and aggression within the previous five years; *or* hold a master's degree or doctorate in psychology, social work, a biological sciences field or a life sciences field with 300 hours in canine behavior consulting on fear, phobias, compulsive behaviors, anxiety and aggression within the previous three years; and submit five references.

- **IAABC:** The International Association of Animal Behavior Consultants was founded in 2004 in recognition that the practice of assisting the public with companion animal behavior problems was a growing field that encompassed many different professionals: veterinarians, animal trainers, animal shelter employees and academics, as well as practicing consultants who didn't always fit neatly into one of the aforementioned categories. The goal of the IAABC is to standardize and support the practice of companion animal behavior consulting, while providing resources for pet owners needing advice. The organization has nearly 1000 members throughout the world (not all members are dog behavior consultants). IAABC members work to minimize the use of aversive stimuli and maximize the effective use of reinforcers to modify animal behavior. The LIMA (least intrusive and minimally aversive) principle is used as a general rule. You must be a member of IAABC to be certified by the organization.

- **CDBC:** The IAABC offers certifications for professionals who do behavior work with a variety of different species. The Certified Dog Behavior Consultant must:
    - Document a minimum of three years and 500 hours experience in animal behavior consulting with client present
    - Complete 400 hours minimum of relevant coursework, seminars and mentorship
    - Submit three written case studies
    - Submit written discussion of four case scenarios and answer questions regarding terminology, techniques, behavior assessment and history taking
    - Possess a minimum educational level of high school diploma or GED
    - Veterinary behaviorists, ACAABs and CAABs are granted membership with the submission of three applicable case studies and the application fee.

- **NADOI:** The National Association of Dog Obedience Instructors was founded in 1965 when a small group of highly experienced dog trainers gathered together and resolved to promote modern, humane training methods, and at the same time elevate the standards of the dog obedience instructing profession. To accomplish these goals, it was decided that members of the organization should be designated as having attained certain skills and knowledge of dog training and obedience instructing. NADOI certified membership requirements include:
    - At least five years' experience in dog obedience training
    - At least two years as a full-charge instructor
    - Past experience working with a minimum of 100 different dogs

   - Submission of training hours (group instructors must have taught at least 104 class hours; private instructors 288 hours)

   - Submission of a written essay that evaluates: knowledge of general dog behavior; ability to deal with specific training problems; knowledge and use of training methods; and teaching and training skills

Although the NADOI "Standards of Conduct" require members to "use and promote humane methods of training" they do not define what those methods are, so much is left to individual interpretation.

Pet Professional Guild

- **PPG:** The Pet Professional Guild is a membership business league for individuals and professional pet industry businesses having the common business interest and goal of furthering the public's education and awareness of force-free dog training and pet care methods and techniques, and the state of research in dog training and pet care. PPG members share the common interest of spreading force-free dog training and pet care methods to the pet industry. The PPG provides professional registry, representation and education to force-free pet care providers and the public with an emphasis on building collaboration among force-free pet trainers and professional pet care providers to improve the business conditions and promote the common interests of force-free animal care and training professionals. The PPG began offering certification in 2015 through the Pet Professional Accreditation Board. The Pet Professional Accreditation Board is operated by the PPG and currently offers two programs: an accreditation for professional canine trainers and an accreditation for canine behavior consultants. Each program has a rigorous path to completion. Applicants are thoroughly tested, both on paper and in practice. Candidates must submit skill videos for assessment. Applicants for the accredited canine behavior consultant will also complete and submit individual case studies. It's not necessary to be a member of PPG to be credentialed through the PPAB, but applicants do have to adhere to PPG's guiding principles which can be viewed here: www.credentialingboard.com/Guiding-Principles

   - **PCT-A:** Professional Canine Trainer (Accredited)

   - **PCBC-A:** Professional Canine Behavior Consultant (Accredited)

- **TDF:** The Truly Dog Friendly (TDF) group is an online list of more than 350 training and behavior professionals who are committed to using dog-friendly methods. TDF defines dog-friendly methods as "reward-based rather than force-based. Dog-friendly trainers do not use shock collars (e-collars), nor do they use coercion, intimidation, or pain. Instead, they teach with a gentle, fair approach so that dogs truly will enjoy learning and form a trusting bond with their owners." TDF does not certify trainers.

Truly Dog Friendly

Training schools with certificate courses

There are many dog training schools that offer certificate courses. While a student who completes one or more courses from these schools may be granted a "certification" title, this type of certification means only that the student passed the course. While some of the courses are very comprehensive, true professional certification tests a broad body of knowledge, not just the knowledge taught in a specific course.

- **CASI:** The Companion Animal Sciences Institute (CASI) provides advanced, challenging, science-based professional development education in the animal behavior, training, behavior change programming, fitness and nutrition fields in an online format. It is the position of CASI that animal-friendly, positive reinforcement–based methods are the most efficient and effective, and least intrusive and risk-laden methods to use in animal training and behavior, and most conducive to facilitating the human-animal bond. Certificate credentials offered by CASI include:
    - **Cert. PDTST:** The Certificate of Professional Dog Training Science and Technology program is a rigorous program of study intended to help the students upgrade and develop important skills for their careers in dog training. It involves an intensive distance course on the principles of learning and the technology of dog training with both academic coursework and hands-on skill practice, and involves hands-on assignments in shaping and chaining techniques.
    - **Cert. SRW:** The Shelter and Rescue Work Certificate program addresses many aspects of working in the dog sheltering and rescue environment. The Shelter and Rescue Work Certificate explores the principles of behavior, domestic behavioral assessment strategies within the shelter environment, training and behavior modification techniques for shelter and rescue environments, disease risk management, environmental enrichment and emotional health management of dogs in shelters, the adoption process itself, and operations of shelters and rescue organizations.

  - **Dip. ABST:** The Diploma of Animal Behavior Science and Technology program addresses key topics in behavior modification and management protocols in great depth including the principles of behavior; tactics, strategies and procedures in non-coercive animal training; functional assessment; behavior modification protocols; professional activities; and professional ethics. Students will have the opportunity to carry out hands-on training with their own companion animal and to engage in a problem behavior resolution project.

- **JDADT:** The Jean Donaldson Academy for Dog Trainers (JDADT) aims to further aversive-free, science-based dog training by making an academically rigorous program available to anyone, no matter where they live, at an affordable cost. This is a comprehensive online program and students can proceed at their own pace. The program can typically be completed in one to two years.

Jean Donaldson Academy for Dog Trainers

- **KPACTP:** The Karen Pryor Academy (KPA) Dog Trainer Professional program takes an innovative approach to developing and supporting outstanding positive reinforcement trainers who teach the general public. Graduates of the academy are Karen Pryor Academy Certified Training Partners (KPACTP). The six-month course combines online learning with hands-on teaching from experienced teachers in the field.

Karen Pryor Academy

- **PPAWS:** Full disclosure...Peaceable Paws (PPAWS), launched in 1996, is my own training business and trainer academy, with a mission to foster harmony between the human and non-human animals of our world. PPaws Academies are intensive, hands-on six-day courses, and graduates of multiple academies are PMCTs (Pat Miller Certified Trainers). The Peaceable Paws Academy has graduated more than 400 trainers since its inception. All PMCTs commit to using force-free methods.

  - **PMCT1:** Level 1 certified trainers have passed the Level 1 Basic Dog Training and Behavior Course, the Level 2 Behavior Modification Course and any third academy.

  - **PMCT2:** Level 2 certified trainers have met the qualifications for PMCT1, and additionally must pass the Level 3 Advanced Training and Behavior Study course. Also, PMCT2s must actively participate in the PMCT2/3 Yahoo! groups list discussing behavior studies, and submit at least 30 CEUs every three years.

- **PMCT3:** Level 3 certified trainers have met the qualifications for PMCT2, including participation on the Yahoo! groups list and submission of CEUs. Additionally, they must complete a fifth academy of their choice, and attend a one-week Private Intern Program with Pat Miller or, alternatively, complete the six- to twelve-month Level 1 Peaceable Paws Apprenticeship.

Peaceable Paws Dog and Puppy Training

Peaceable Paws Academy for Dog Trainers

- **VSPDT:** Victoria Stilwell Positively Dog Training (VSPDT) is a global network of professional dog trainers committed to promoting positive reinforcement methodologies. VSPDT just started offering a dog trainer school in the spring of 2016 as this book was being written, and licenses as VSPDT trainers those who: are currently practicing professional dog trainers; employ only positive reinforcement dog training philosophies in all practices; avoid dominance-based alpha-hierarchy methodologies in all practices; can show proof of current dog trainer's liability insurance coverage; are available for a one-hour phone consultation with a Victoria Stilwell Positively application processor; are willing to undergo a dog training evaluation by Victoria and her team; and are prepared to purchase a Victoria Stilwell Positively Dog Training License.

Glossary

Affiliative behavior: any behavior that is offered with the intent of supporting or improving one's individual relationship with others

Agonistic: pertaining to the range of activities associated with aggressive encounters between members of the same species (other dogs) or social group (can include humans and other animals), including threat, attack, appeasement or retreat

Alpha roll: flipping a dog on his back and pinning him down until he stops struggling (not recommended!)

Antecedent: whatever occurs prior to the behavior that causes the behavior to happen

Anxiety: the distress or uneasiness of mind caused by apprehensive anticipation of *pending* danger or misfortune, real or imagined

Balanced training: a training philosophy open to using the full spectrum of training tools and methods, not exclusively force-free methods (not recommended)

Baseline distance: in the CAT procedure, that distance at which the dog is aware of the presence of the aversive stimulus without being over threshold—the distance at which the CAT work begins

BAT (Behavioral Adjustment Training): with BAT, the aversive target is stationary, and the subject dog moves toward it at his own pace. If the dog gives a cut-off signal, he is allowed or prompted to move away from the target as a reward

CAT (Constructional Aggression Treatment): a behavior modification protocol that uses operant conditioning (negative reinforcement) to teach a dog a new behavior in place of his fear-related aggression

Clicker training: positive reinforcement training that uses a marker signal to tell the dog when he has performed a behavior that earns a treat

Conditioned emotional response (CER): the physical manifestation of your dog's new association with the stimulus

Conditioned reinforcer: something the dog *learns* has value through its association with a primary reinforcer (clicker makes treats happen—food is a primary reinforcer, the clicker is a conditioned reinforcer)

Consequence: how behavior is impacted—either a good thing happens (is reinforcing and tends to increase) or a bad thing happens (is punishing and tends to decrease)

Counter-conditioning and desensitization: giving your dog a new association—usually giving him a positive association with something he dislikes or is afraid of, starting with a low intensity of stimulus and gradually working up to full intensity of stimulus

Crossover trainer: a trainer who originally trained using old-fashioned force-based methods and who no longer uses those methods, and is now proud to promote positive reinforcement–based training

Cuffing: hitting the dog under the chin with an open hand (not recommended)

Cut-off signal: body language that tells the handler the dog would prefer to increase distance from the scary thing, such as sniffing the ground or looking back at the handler

Dominance theory: a theory developed from a flawed study of captive wolves in which the scientist concluded that wolves in a pack fight to gain dominance, and the winner is the alpha wolf

Fear: a feeling of apprehension associated with the actual presence or proximity of an object, individual or social situation perceived as a threat

Flooding: presenting an aversive stimulus at full intensity until the subject dog reaches a level of learned helplessness, gives up and shuts down (not recommended)

Force-free training: a training philosophy that values partnership and voluntary cooperation with the dog and eschews the use of tools and techniques that utilize pain, coercion or fear

Generalization: helping the dog understand that the behavior, training or modification process works everywhere, not just in the original training environment

Greedy trainer syndrome: trying to do too much too quickly in your training or behavior modification program

Idiopathic: of, relating to, or designating a disease having no known cause

Management: the process of arranging a dog's environment to prevent opportunity for aggressive behavior

Modification: changing the dog's behavioral and emotional responses to stimuli that cause aggression so the dog no longer feels the need to aggress.

Negative punishment: the subject's behavior makes a *good* thing go away, so the behavior decreases

Negative reinforcement: the subject's behavior makes a *bad* thing go away, so the behavior increases

Operant: making a deliberate behavior choice in expectation of consequences

Operant conditioning: using delivery and removal of reinforcers and punishers to train behaviors

Paradoxical effect: when a medication has the opposite behavioral effect from what was intended

Phobia: persistent, extreme, inappropriate fear or anxiety responses, far out of proportion to the level or nature of threat presented

Piloerection: hair on the dog's neck and back stands up—evidence of excitement, arousal or aggression

Positive punishment: the subject's behavior makes a *bad* thing happen, so the behavior decreases

Positive reinforcement: the subject's behavior makes a *good* thing happen, so the behavior increases

Positive reinforcement training: training that reinforces appropriate/desired behavior and does not use force, coercion or fear to extinguish unwanted behavior

Primary reinforcer: something that has innate value, such as food—the dog doesn't have to *learn* that it has value

Priming: doing something your dog loves in order to get his brain in a happy place to help him be better able to handle potentially distressing events

Scruff shake: grab both sides of the dog's face and shake, lifting the dog off the ground (not recommended)

Shutting down behavior: using positive punishment or flooding to convince a dog that it's not safe to do anything unless instructed to do something (not recommended)

Socialization: helping your young dog learn that the world is a safe and happy place through careful exposure to all kinds of different people, places and things

Stimulus: the thing that causes a behavioral response

Switchover: in the CAT procedure, when the subject dog begins offering affiliative (friendly) body language signals to the previously aversive stimulus

Targeting: teaching your dog to touch a designated body part to a designated target

Trigger stacking: the compilation of multiple stressors that serves to put a dog over his bite threshold

Whale eye: white sclera of the dog's eye is visible around iris. May be due to stress and part of an agonistic warning, or may simply be that the dog's nose is pointed a different direction from his eyes

Recommended Books and DVDs

Books

Aggressive Behavior in Dogs. A Comprehensive Technical Manual for Professionals, 2nd edition. James O'Heare, 2014. Very complete and technical volume for behavior professionals who are serious about their knowledge and education.

Behavior Adjustment Training 2.0. Grisha Stewart, 2016. Stewart's new version of the BAT procedure, which gives the subject dog even more freedom of choice and movement.

The Cautious Canine. How to Help Dogs Conquer Their Fears, 2nd edition. Patricia McConnell, 2005. Small, easy-to-read booklet on working with a fearful dog.

Control Unleashed. Creating a Focused and Confident Dog. Leslie McDevitt, 2007. Learn how to turn stress into confidence and distraction into focus using positive methods.

Dogs are From Neptune. Jean Donaldson, 1998. Case histories illustrate protocols for modifying aggressive behavior using counter-conditioning and desensitization, in an easy-to-read Q&A format.

Dogs Bite but Balloons and Slippers Are More Dangerous. Janis Bradley, 2005. Dogs enhance the lives of millions more people than even the most inflated estimates of dog-bite victims. Gain a new perspective on this issue and learn strategies to minimize the number of bites that do occur.

Dominance in Dogs; Fact or Fiction. Barry Eaton, 2011. This book separates out the facts from the fiction regarding dominance in pet dogs, presenting the results of recent research into the behavior of wolves and the impacts of selective breeding on the behavior of dogs.

Dominance Theory and Dogs, 2nd edition. James O'Heare, 2008. An exploration of the theory of dominance and how it applies to domestic dogs.

Don't Shoot the Dog. Karen Pryor, 1999. Despite its name, this is not exclusively a dog training book. In addition to being effective for training dogs, the behavioral training techniques presented can work on people and other animals as well.

Feisty Fido. Help for the Leash Reactive Dog, 2nd edition. Patricia McConnell and Karen London, 2009. Small, easy-to-read booklet on working with a reactive dog.

Help for Your Fearful Dog. A Step-by-Step Guide for Helping Your Dog Conquer His Fears. Nicole Wilde, 2006. A comprehensive guide to the treatment of canine anxiety, fears, and phobias.

Manual of Clinical Behavioral Medicine for Dogs and Cats. Karen Overall, 2013. This is an in-depth college textbook-level excellent resource—everything you could possibly want to know about dog and cat behavior. Includes a CD with behavior modification protocols."

Mine! A Practical Guide to Resource Guarding in Dogs. Jean Donaldson, 2002. A practical how-to guide on resource guarding—food bowl, object, bed, crate, owner, etc.—in dogs.

DVDs/Apps/Videos

Body Language

The Dog Decoder (App). Jill Breitner, *www.dogdecoder.com.* Canine body language can be confusing, but with the help of Dog Decoder, you'll learn to understand any dog's signals like a pro.

The Language of Dogs. Understanding Canine Body Language and Other Communication Signals (DVD). Sarah Kalnajs, CPDT-KA, CDBC, 2006. Extensive footage of various dog breeds and hundreds of examples of canine behavior, body language and other communication signals.

Constructional Aggression Treatment (CAT)

Constructional Aggression Treatment; C.A.T. for Dogs (DVD). Jesus Rosales Ruiz and Kellie Snider, 2009. In-depth discussion of this procedure by the creators of C.A.T.

Juni's C.A.T. Procedure (DVD) Pat Miller, 2008. See how C.A.T. can change the behavior—and life—of a dog with serious behavior challenges, and of the human who loves him. *www.youtube.com/watch?v=XdnED053tDw,* CAT video with Dr. Jesus Rosales Ruiz and Kellie Snider

Behavior Adjustment Training (BAT)

www.youtube.com/watch?v=yPYI7zn2eIU, BAT video, Sean Howard/Up With Pup

Talking Dogs

www.youtube.com/watch?v=bFsR772EByQ, Dogs who have been taught to make sounds that sound like words.

Drop It

www.youtube.com/watch?v=ndTiVOCNY4M, "Drop It" protocol with Chirag Patel

Acepromazine

www.youtube.com/watch?v=6-GsmrFYHKk, Why not to use acepromazine with Dr. Karen Overall

Other Resources

Products:

Adaptil: *www.adaptil.com*

Chase and Chomp Sticky Bone: *www.caitec.com/product-p/711085600527.htm*

Tethers: *www.baddogsinc.com/product/regular-tethers*

Thundershirt: *www.thundershirt.com*

Through a Dog's Ear: *www.throughadogsear.com*

Websites:

American College of Veterinary Behavior: *www.dacvb.org*

American Veterinary Society of Animal Behavior: *www.avsabonline.org*

AVSAB Statement on Puppy Socialization: *www.avsabonline.org/uploads/position_statements/puppy_socialization1-25-13.pdf*

Animal Behavior Society: *www.animalbehaviorsociety.org*

Association of Animal Behavior Professionals: *www.associationofanimalbehavior-professionals.com*

Association of Professional Dog Trainers (US): *www.apdt.com*

Association of Pet Dog Trainers (Australia): *www.apdt.com.au*

Association of Professional Dog Trainers (Canada): *www.cappdt.ca*

Association of Pet Dog Trainers (NZ): *www.apdtnz.org.nz*

Association of Pet Dog Trainers (UK): *www.apdt.co.uk*

Certification Council for Professional Dog Trainers: *www.ccpdt.org*

Companion Animal Sciences Institute: *www.casinstitute.com*

International Association of Animal Behavior Consultants: *www.iaabc.org*

Jean Donaldson Academy for Dog Trainers: *www.academyfordogtrainers.com*

Karen Pryor: *www.karenpryoracademy.com*

Peaceable Paws (Pat Miller) Trainer Academies: *www.peaceablepaws.com*

Pet Professional Guild: *www.petprofessionalguild.com*

Treat and Retreat: *www.dogstardaily.com/training/retreat-treat*

Treat and Retreat: *www.suzanneclothier.com*

Victoria Stilwell Academy: *www.positively.com*

About the Author

Dogs and dog training have been a consistent theme throughout Pat Miller's life. Beginning at age six with the family Beagle, Flag, continuing in her teenage years when she showed her Rough Collie, Squire, and into her professional life, Pat has enthusiastically shared her world and her heart with dogs. She has titled her canine companions in Obedience and Rally, trained dogs in a wide variety of dog sports and built her career around animals. Pat is an internationally acclaimed speaker, was named in the spring of 2015 by Dog Fancy magazine as one of 45 people who have changed the dog world, and is training editor and a columnist for *Whole Dog Journal.* Pat is the author of: *The Power of Positive Dog Training; Positive Perspectives—Love Your Dog, Train Your Dog; Positive Perspectives 2—Love Your Dog, Know Your Dog; Play with Your Dog; Do Over Dogs;* and *How to Foster Dogs.*

Working now with people and their dogs, Pat has her own training establishment, Peaceable Paws, LLC, on 80 acres near Hagerstown, Maryland, where she offers dog trainer academies and workshops, dog training classes and one-to-one behavior consulting to pet dog owners as well as horse boarding services.

Peaceable Paws also hosts a number of courses and programs for both the professional dog trainer and those wanting to become a professional. Pat is past president of the Association of Professional Dog Trainers (APDT), the largest professional organization for dog trainers in the world; a past board member for the Certification Council for Professional Dog Trainers; and a Certified Behavior Consultant, Canine (CBCC-KA) and Certified Professional Dog Trainer (CPDT-KA).

As a 20-year veteran of the Marin Humane Society in California, Pat knows too well that aggressive behavior in dogs can have tragic endings. She and her husband live with their canine, feline, porcine and equine family in Fairplay, Maryland. Learn more about Pat and her programs at www.peaceablepaws.com.

INDEX

Also available from Dogwise Publishing

Go to www.dogwise.com for more books and ebooks.

AGGRESSION IN DOGS

Practical Management, Prevention and Behaviour Modification

Brenda Aloff

Brenda Aloff's book has become the bible for identifying, understanding, and resolving aggression problems in dogs. Contains detailed training protocols to use in specific types of aggression situations and how to manage the aggressive dog for his safety and the community's. As the book says, aggression has a wide range of manifestations. And, it shows how to address reactive or aggressive behavior, with over 400 pages of text, drawings, and photographs.

SCAREDY DOG

Understanding and Rehabilitating Your Reactive Dog

Ali Brown

When dogs growl at other dogs, lunge at people and bark at everything it's often mislabeled as "aggression." But behavior that looks like aggression is often fear-based and should be treated as such. The appropriate term for this constellation of behaviors is "reactivity." This book helps dog owners and trainers to understand the reactive dog and help him change for the better. Easy to read and understand, with photographs and graphics to help you improve behavior and solve problems.

FEISTY FIDO

Help for the Leash Reactive Dog, 2nd Ed.

Patricia McConnell and Karen London

Do you have a Jekyll and Hyde dog at the other end of the leash? Is she wonderful with familiar dogs but barks and lunges at unfamiliar ones? Because of this book, thousands of people can now enjoy being out and about with their dogs instead of being anxious and nervous. Feisty Fido provides practical information about positive training ways to teach dogs how to politely walk past other dogs without causing a scene.

AGGRESSIVE BEHAVIOR IN DOGS

A Comprehensive Technical Manual for Professionals, 2nd Ed.

James O'Heare

A comprehensive technical manual, written for dog behavior professionals. How to assess the problem, constructing systematic behavior change programs, and case management techniques. The new second edition features a more behavioral approach to the prevention and assessment of aggression in dogs and strategies to help professionals solve aggression problems brought to them by their clients.

BEHAVIOR ADJUSTMENT TRAINING 2.0

Grisha Stewart, M.A., CPDT-KA

With *BAT 2.0,* trainer/author Grisha Stewart has completely overhauled Behavior Adjustment Training (BAT) to create a new efficient and practical tool for dog reactivity. *BAT 2.0* builds resilience and self-reliance by giving dogs safe opportunities to learn about people, dogs, or other "triggers." Clear enough for all readers to follow, this book also includes technical tips and bonus chapters just for dog behavior professionals. Learn how to rehabilitate aggression, frustration and fear. Grisha will teach you how to apply her technique to all dogs and puppies—and get your life back!

FIGHT!

A Practical Guide to the Treatment of Dog-Dog Aggression

Jean Donaldson

Fight! by Jean Donaldson is a practical guide to the treatment of dog-dog aggression. This down-to-earth manual will teach you how to use behavior modification to retrain a dog that bullies other dogs or becomes fearful when approached by other dogs. This down-to-earth manual will teach you how to use behavior modification to retrain a dog that bullies other dogs, or becomes fearful when approached by other dogs.

Printed in Great Britain
by Amazon

72705775R00120